2020 - 2021

by **ARGO
BROTHERS**

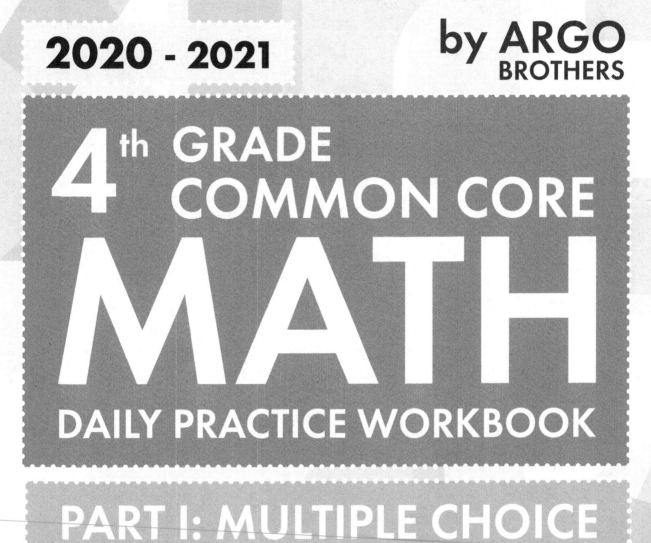

4th GRADE
Common Core
MATH

DAILY PRACTICE WORKBOOK

PART I: MULTIPLE CHOICE

ARGOPREP.COM

FREE **ONLINE SYSTEM
WITH VIDEO
EXPLANATIONS**

ArgoPrep is one of the leading providers of supplemental educational products and services. We offer affordable and effective test prep solutions to educators, parents and students. Learning should be fun and easy! For that reason, most of our workbooks come with detailed video answer explanations taught by one of our fabulous instructors.

Our goal is to make your life easier, so let us know how we can help you by e-mailing us at: info@argoprep.com.

Aknowlegments:
Icons made by Freepik, Creaticco Creative Agency, Pixel perfect , Pixel Buddha, Smashicons, Twitter , Good Ware, Smalllikeart, Nikita Golubev, monkik, DinosoftLabs, Icon Pond from www.flaticon.com

TABLE OF CONTENTS

HOW TO USE
THE BOOK

This workbook is designed to give lots of practice with the math Common Core State Standards (CCSS). By practicing and mastering this entire workbook, your child will become very familiar and comfortable with the state math exam. If you are a teacher using this workbook for your students, you will notice each question is labeled with the specific standard so you can easily assign your students problems in the workbook. This workbook takes the CCSS and divides them up among 20 weeks. By working on these problems on a daily basis, students will be able to (1) find any deficiencies in their understanding and/or practice of math and (2) have small successes each day that will build proficiency and confidence in their abilities.

We strongly recommend watching the videos as it will reinforce the fundamental concepts. Please note, scrap paper may be necessary while using this workbook so that the student has sufficient space to show their work.

For a detailed overview of the Common Core State Standards for 4th grade, please visit: www.corestandards.org/Math/Content/4/introduction/

HOW TO WATCH
VIDEO EXPLANATIONS
IT IS ABSOLUTELY FREE

Download our app:
ArgoPrep Video Explanations
to access videos on any mobile device or tablet.

or

Step 1 - Visit our website at: www.argoprep.com/k8
Step 2 - Click on the "Video Explanations button located on the top right corner.
Step 3 - Choose the workbook you have and enjoy video explanations.

Let's Begin!

OTHER BOOKS BY ARGOPREP

Here are some other test prep workbooks by ArgoPrep you may be interested in. All of our workbooks come equipped with detailed video explanations to make your learning experience a breeze! Visit us at **www.argoprep.com**

COMMON CORE MATH SERIES

COMMON CORE ELA SERIES

INTRODUCING MATH!

Introducing Math! by ArgoPrep is an award-winning series created by certified teachers to provide students with high-quality practice problems. Our workbooks include topic overviews with instruction, practice questions, answer explanations along with digital access to video explanations. Practice in confidence - with ArgoPrep!

SCIENCE SERIES

Science Daily Practice Workbook by ArgoPrep is an award-winning series created by certified science teachers to help build mastery of foundational science skills. Our workbooks explore science topics in depth with ArgoPrep s 5 E S to build science mastery.

KIDS SUMMER ACADEMY SERIES

ArgoPrep's **Kids Summer Academy** series helps prevent summer learning loss and gets students ready for their new school year by reinforcing core foundations in math, english and science. Our workbooks also introduce new concepts so students can get a head start and be on top of their game for the new school year!

SUMMER ACTIVITY PLAYGROUND SERIES

Summer Activity Playground is another summer series that is designed to prevent summer learning loss and prepares students for the new school year. Students will be able to practice math, ELA, science, social studies and more! This is a new released series that offers the latest aligned learning standards for each grade.

For more practice with 4th Grade Math, be sure to check out our other book
Common Core Math Workbook Grade 4: Free Response

WEEK 1

VIDEO EXPLANATIONS ▶ ARGOPREP.COM

Week 1 is all about numbers – their names, their values and different ways of writing them. You'll also learn how to compare them using comparison symbols such as greater than (>), less than (<) and equal to (=).

You can find detailed video explanations of each problem in the book by visiting:
ArgoPrep.com

WEEK I : DAY I

1. In the number 412,669, how many times greater is the value represented by the 6 in the hundreds place than the value represented by the 6 in the tens place?

   A. 10
   B. 100
   C. 1000
   D. 10,000

   4.NBT.1

2. In which of the following pairs of numbers is the value of 7 in the first number ten times the value of 7 in the second number?

   A. 712 and 37
   B. 870 and 714
   C. 971 and 617
   D. 7,028 and 6,971

   4.NBT.1

3. The 4 in 429 is how many times bigger than the 4 in 514?

   A. 10
   B. 100
   C. 1000
   D. 10,000

   4.NBT.1

4. Ashton wrote a number that used the digit 3 twice in the number. One of the digits of 3 is written so that it is 10 times the other digit of 3. Which number could be Ashton's number?

   A. 36,413
   B. 32,350
   C. 15,363
   D. 73,308

   4.NBT.1

5. Choose the number pair that has digits of 9 that differ in place by a factor of 1,000.

   A. 9,000 and 90
   B. 319 and 499
   C. 5,690 and 19,723
   D. 91,576 and 4,092

   4.NBT.1

6. The 8 in 87,012 is how many times greater than the 8 in 16,840?

   A. 10
   B. 100
   C. 1000
   D. 10,000

   4.NBT.1

TIP of the DAY

Don't forget that a 6 in the hundreds place is 6 *hundreds* (600) and that a 6 in the tens place is 6 *tens* (60).

WEEK 1 : DAY 2

1. The 4 in 4,012 is how many times bigger than the 4 in 6,834?

   A. 10
   B. 100
   C. 1000
   D. 10,000

   4.NBT.1

2. In which of the following pairs of numbers is the value of 5 in the first number one hundred times the value of 5 in the second number?

   A. 512 and 375
   B. 457 and 562
   C. 715 and 953
   D. 15,264 and 6,508

   4.NBT.1

3. The 2 in 2,807 is how many times bigger than the 2 in 8,462?

   A. 10
   B. 100
   C. 1000
   D. 10,000

   4.NBT.1

4. Which number has a 6 that represents a value ten times greater than the value represented by the 6 in 16,523?

   A. 56,713
   B. 15,652
   C. 18,560
   D. 65,142

   4.NBT.1

5. The 4 in 4,129 is how many times bigger than the 4 in 5,437?

   A. 10
   B. 100
   C. 1000
   D. 10,000

   4.NBT.1

6. Choose the number pair that has digits of 8 that differ in place by a factor of 100.

   A. 9,802 and 810
   B. 8,719 and 4,819
   C. 5,890 and 8,725
   D. 81,576 and 4,832

   4.NBT.1

TIP of the DAY

Remember that if the same number is in the hundreds and thousands place, the digit in the thousands place is ten times the digit in the hundreds place. So 7,000 is ten times as much as 700.

1. Which of these numbers is the greatest?

   A. 5,680
   B. 8,416
   C. 5,874
   D. 4,972

   4.NBT.2

2. Which number sentence below is true?

   A. 836 > 874
   B. 129 < 130
   C. 1370 = 1307
   D. 742 < 741

   4.NBT.2

3. Which expression represents the number four thousand, three hundred sixty-two written in expanded form?

   A. 4000 + 300 + 60 + 2
   B. 4000 + 300 + 62
   C. 400 + 300 + 60 + 2
   D. 40,000 + 360 + 2

   4.NBT.2

4. Duncan is given this number: 400,000 + 60,000 + 700 + 10 + 3. Which number below is Duncan's number?

   A. 460,703   C. 46,713
   B. 467,103   D. 460,713

   4.NBT.2

5. Five schools counted their library books, and the number of books are shown below.

School	Number of Books
West Bend	956,031
Eastlane	971,452
Southside	975,380
Northern	968,126
Central	970,883

   Which school had more books than Eastlane?

   A. West Bend   C. Northern
   B. Southside   D. Central

   4.NBT.2

6. Which number is fourteen thousand, six?

   A. 14,060
   B. 1,406
   C. 14,006
   D. 40,006

   4.NBT.2

TIP of the DAY

Don't forget that < means less than so 56 < 65.

WEEK 1 : DAY 4

1. Which number is fifty-eight thousand, two hundred seventy-one when written in expanded form?

   A. 58,000 + 200 + 70 + 1
   B. 48,000 + 200 + 70 + 1
   C. 50,000 + 8,000 + 200 + 71
   D. 50,000 + 8,000 + 200 + 70 + 1

   4.NBT.2

2. Which of these numbers is the smallest?

   A. 49,187
   B. 49,205
   C. 49,109
   D. 49,762

   4.NBT.2

3. What number is the same as 700,000 + 10,000 + 3,000 + 20 + 3?

   A. 701,323
   B. 71,323
   C. 713,203
   D. 713,023

   4.NBT.2

4. Which number sentence below is true?

   A. 1134 = 722 + 412
   B. 5129 < 5129
   C. 315 + 383 = 678
   D. 287 > 951 − 438

   4.NBT.2

5. Which number is sixteen thousand, five hundred twelve in expanded form?

   A. 10,000 + 6,000 + 500 + 10 + 2
   B. 16,000 + 512
   C. 60,000 + 500 + 10 + 2
   D. 16,000 + 500 + 12

   4.NBT.2

6. The distance between Middle University (MU) and four cities is shown below.

City	Distance (miles)
Columbus	315.9
Springfield	472.8
Madison	458
Oakville	501.6

   According to the chart, which statement below is true?

   A. Columbus is farther from MU than Madison.
   B. Oakville is the furthest from MU.
   C. Madison is closer to MU than Columbus.
   D. Springfield is closer to MU than Madison.

   4.NBT.2

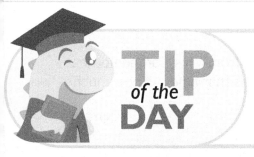

TIP *of the* **DAY**

Tomorrow when you take the assessment, remember to take one question at a time and check every answer choice.

15

1. Choose the number pair that has digits of 4 that differ in place by a factor of 1000.

   A. 49,823 and 81,540
   B. 83,419 and 46,859
   C. 54,890 and 81,745
   D. 47,063 and 54,722

   4.NBT.1

4. Which number is three hundred forty thousand, six hundred seventeen in expanded form?

   A. 300,000 + 4,000 + 600 + 10 + 7
   B. 300,000 + 40,000 + 600 + 10 + 7
   C. 340,000 + 600 + 10 + 7
   D. 30,000 + 4,000 + 600 + 10 + 7

   4.NBT.2

2. Which number sentence below is true?

   A. 651,072 < 650,980
   B. 16,934 = 16,943
   C. 414,989 < 413,999
   D. 12,652 > 12,562

   4.NBT.2

5. Which of these numbers is the largest?

   A. 153,981
   B. 152,998
   C. 153,987
   D. 153,900

   4.NBT.2

3. The 5 in 54,109 is how many times bigger than the 5 in 75,430?

   A. 10
   B. 100
   C. 1000
   D. 10,000

   4.NBT.1

6. Choose the number pair that has digits of 7 that differ in place by a factor of 100.

   A. 970,862 and 657,412
   B. 12,587,004 and 4,735,908
   C. 703,125 and 819,527
   D. 94,376 and 76,890

   4.NBT.1

DAY 6
Challenge question

Chris inherited $5,000 from his grandmother. If Brooke received ten times that amount, how much money did she receive?

4.NBT.2

16

WEEK 2

VIDEO EXPLANATIONS

ARGOPREP.COM

This week we are going to practice rounding numbers. Rounding is useful when you don't need an exact number, but you need a rough estimate. You'll have the opportunity to add and subtract lots of numbers.

You can find detailed video explanations of each problem in the book by visiting:
ArgoPrep.com

1. What is 2,649 rounded to the nearest ten?

   A. 2,650
   B. 2,600
   C. 3,000
   D. 2,640

   4.NBT.3

4. Paul had $12,984 in his account for college. What is 12,984 rounded to the nearest hundred?

   A. 13,000
   B. 12,900
   C. 12,980
   D. 10,000

   4.NBT.3

2. What is 6,812,783 rounded to the nearest thousand?

   A. 6,812,800
   B. 6,800,000
   C. 6,810,000
   D. 6,813,000

   4.NBT.3

5. Round 4,096,154 to the nearest ten thousand.

   A. 4,190,000
   B. 4,100,000
   C. 4,096,000
   D. 4,096,200

   4.NBT.3

3. What is 7,512,745 rounded to the nearest hundred-thousand?

   A. 7,510,000
   B. 7,513,000
   C. 7,500,000
   D. 7,600,000

   4.NBT.3

6. What is 8,362,587 rounded to the nearest million?

   A. 8,363,000
   B. 8,360,000
   C. 8,400,000
   D. 8,000,000

   4.NBT.3

TIP *of the* **DAY**

When rounding, remember if it is 5 or higher, we round UP. Rounding 45,316 to the tens place would give us 45,320.

1. What is 647,380 rounded to the nearest ten?

   A. 647,380
   B. 647,400
   C. 647,000
   D. 650,000

   4.NBT.3

2. What is 5,601,387 rounded to the nearest thousand?

   A. 5,601,390
   B. 5,601,400
   C. 5,601,000
   D. 5,600,000

   4.NBT.3

3. Which number is thirty-three thousand, two?

   A. 3,302
   B. 330,002
   C. 33,002
   D. 30,302

   4.NBT.2

4. What is 1,384 rounded to the nearest ten?

   A. 1,390
   B. 1,380
   C. 1,400
   D. 1,000

   4.NBT.3

5. Cars were for sale at the Cool-Cars-4-U car lot. The lot was divided into 4 sections and the number of cars in each section is shown below.

Lot	Number of Cars
A	4,349
B	5,601
C	4,087
D	4,622

   Which lot could be rounded to 5000?

   A. Lot A
   B. Lot B
   C. Lot C
   D. Lot D

   4.NBT.3

TIP of the DAY

When rounding, if the number we are looking for is 4 or less, we do NOT round down. The number will remain the SAME.

19

1. What is 367 + 504?

   A. 771
   B. 871
   C. 971
   D. 979

   4.NBT.4

2. Which pair of numbers have a sum of 4,682?

   A. 2,000 and 2,286
   B. 4,000 and 862
   C. 3,200 and 1,482
   D. 2,600 and 1,082

   4.NBT.4

3. What is the difference between 987 and 452?

   A. 425
   B. 435
   C. 535
   D. 635

   4.NBT.4

4. What is 5,281 – 3,714?

   A. 1548
   B. 1567
   C. 1573
   D. 1678

   4.NBT.4

5. Which number sentence below is true?

   A. 4892 – 1367 = 3535
   B. 5175 + 2926 = 7101
   C. 8413 – 5573 = 3740
   D. 7984 + 1202 = 9186

   4.NBT.4

6. Ava and her brother collect pennies. Ava started with 1,289 pennies and then her brother gave her his collection of 835 pennies. Now how many pennies does Ava have?

   A. 454
   B. 554
   C. 8,478
   D. 2,124

   4.NBT.4

TIP of the DAY

When adding or subtracting, remember to line up the place values so you are adding (or subtracting) ones with ones, tens with tens, etc.

1. In 156,443 how many times greater is the number 4 in the hundreds place than the number 4 in the tens place?

   A. 1
   B. 10
   C. 100
   D. 1000

   4.NBT.1

2. Which number sentence below is true?

   A. $4800 - 1537 = 3267$
   B. $1655 + 704 = 951$
   C. $983 - 597 = 386$
   D. $843 + 3942 = 4875$

   4.NBT.4

3. Which pair of numbers have a sum of 837?

   A. 356 and 421
   B. 493 and 464
   C. 715 and 132
   D. 572 and 265

   4.NBT.4

4. Ben had 6,217 building blocks. If he gave 2,980 to his sister, how many did Ben have left?

   A. 3,133
   B. 3,237
   C. 4,773
   D. 9,197

   4.NBT.4

5. The number of marbles 4 students had is shown below.

Student	Marbles
Bryan	349
Connor	512
Evelyn	499
Olivia	382

   According to the chart, which 2 students would have 881 marbles if they combined theirs?

   A. Bryan and Connor
   B. Evelyn and Olivia
   C. Bryan and Olivia
   D. Connor and Evelyn

   4.NBT.4

TIP of the DAY

Tomorrow when you take the assessment, don't forget to double check your answers.

WEEK 2 : DAY 5

1. What is the sum of 4517 and 3635?

   A. 7,143
   B. 7,152
   C. 7,953
   D. 8,152

   4.NBT.4

2. Which number could be rounded to 7,000?

   A. 6,275
   B. 6,498
   C. 7,176
   D. 7,504

   4.NBT.3

3. What is 546,419 rounded to the nearest thousand?

   A. 546,420
   B. 546,000
   C. 547,000
   D. 550,000

   4.NBT.3

4. Kari had driven her car 48,952 miles. Round 48,952 to the nearest hundred.

   A. 48,000
   B. 48,900
   C. 48,950
   D. 49,000

   4.NBT.3

5. Which of these numbers is the same as 50,749?

   A. 5 ten thousands + 7 hundreds + 4 tens + 9 ones
   B. 5 thousands + 7 hundreds + 4 tens + 9 ones
   C. 5 ten thousands + 7 thousands + 4 hundreds + 9 ones
   D. 50 thousands + 7 hundreds + 49 tens

   4.NBT.2

6. What is 9,700 – 926?

   A. 440
   B. 8,226
   C. 8,676
   D. 8,774

   4.NBT.4

DAY 6
Challenge question

What is 972 + 1683? Take that sum and round to the nearest hundred. What number do you get?

4.NBT.3
4.NBT.4

WEEK 3

ARGOPREP.COM

VIDEO ▶
EXPLANATIONS

Week 3 has lots of division problems. Sometimes numbers go into other numbers "evenly" and sometimes there are remainders (or leftovers). Week 3 will provide lots of practice using division.

You can find detailed video explanations of each problem in the book by visiting:
ArgoPrep.com

1. Find the product of 47 and 12.

   A. 634
   B. 564
   C. 59
   D. 35

   4.NBT.5

2. There were 8 boxes that each contained 105 shirts. How many shirts were in the boxes?

   A. 815
   B. 830
   C. 840
   D. 855

   4.NBT.5

3. What is 3,892 times 6?

   A. 22,462
   B. 22,892
   C. 23,352
   D. 23,462

   4.NBT.5

4. The stadium had a section that had 9 seats in each row and contained 412 rows. How many seats were in that section?

   A. 3,498
   B. 3,578
   C. 3,608
   D. 3,708

   4.NBT.5

5. What is 16 × 52?

   A. 732
   B. 782
   C. 832
   D. 852

   4.NBT.5

6. Which expression can be used to find 45 times 12?

   A. (45 × 10) + (45 × 2)
   B. (45 × 10) + (5 × 2)
   C. (40 × 10) + (5 × 2)
   D. (40 × 2) + (5 × 10)

   4.NBT.5

TIP of the DAY

When multiplying, don't forget that place value is important. If you are multiplying a number by 30, you are not multiplying by 3, you are multiplying by 3 tens.

1. There are 25 rolls of carpeting on each shelf. How many rolls of carpet are on 13 shelves?

   A. 279
   B. 312
   C. 325
   D. 335

   4.NBT.5

2. Find the product of 7 and 518.

   A. 3,616
   B. 3,626
   C. 3,636
   D. 3,646

   4.NBT.5

3. Which expression can be used to find 72 times 35?

   A. $(70 \times 5) + (2 \times 30)$
   B. $(3 \times 72) + (5 \times 72)$
   C. $(30 \times 70) + (5 \times 2)$
   D. $(30 \times 72) + (5 \times 72)$

   4.NBT.5

4. What is 14 times 22?

   A. 56
   B. 248
   C. 288
   D. 308

   4.NBT.5

5. Which expression is the same as $(21 \times 80) + (21 \times 3)$?

   A. 83×21
   B. $21 \times 80 \times 3$
   C. $8 \times 21 \times 3$
   D. $3 \times 80 \times 21$

   4.NBT.5

6. Which statement below is true?

   A. $412 + 33 = 500 - 55$
   B. $6 \times 17 = 16 \times 7$
   C. $329 - 16 < 218 + 35$
   D. $62 \times 32 > 73 \times 45$

   4.NBT.2

TIP of the DAY

It is always good to take a break when you are studying for a long time. You can take a quick walk, stretch, or grab a glass of water. Taking a break allows your brain to learn better.

1. What is 782 divided by 5?

   A. 156
   B. 156 r 2
   C. 156 r 3
   D. 156 r 4

   4.NBT.6

4. What is 1486 + 7325?

   A. 7811
   B. 8811
   C. 8981
   D. 9001

   4.NBT.4

2. When 507 is divided by 9, what is the remainder?

   A. 1
   B. 2
   C. 3
   D. 5

   4.NBT.6

5. What is the quotient when 1,248 is divided by 4?

   A. 123
   B. 213
   C. 273
   D. 312

   4.NBT.6

3. The store has 583 cans of paint. If a shelf can hold 6 cans of paint, how many shelves would be needed to hold all of the paint?

   A. 95
   B. 96
   C. 97
   D. 98

   4.NBT.6

6. Kim found 350 pieces of paper. If she can fit 7 pieces of paper in one envelope, how many envelopes would she need?

   A. 5
   B. 50
   C. 500
   D. 5,000

   4.NBT.6

TIP of the DAY

When dividing, be careful to keep your numbers in the correct column so the numbers have the right value.

WEEK 3 : DAY 4

1. What is 5,614 divided by 3?

   A. 1781 r 2
   B. 1871 r 1
   C. 1891 r 2
   D. 1921 r 1

   4.NBT.6

2. Which number sentence below is true?

   A. 3457 ÷ 8 = 432 r 1
   B. 3457 ÷ 7 = 490 r 1
   C. 3457 ÷ 6 = 574 r 1
   D. 3457 ÷ 5 = 692 r 1

   4.NBT.6

3. If there are 510 pairs of shoes in 6 crates, how many pairs are in each crate?

   A. 81
   B. 83
   C. 85
   D. 87

   4.NBT.6

4. What is the quotient when 3677 is divided by 8?

   A. 458 r 3
   B. 459 r 5
   C. 460 r 2
   D. 461 r 7

   4.NBT.6

5. What is the expanded form of fifty thousand, two hundred forty-nine?

   A. 5 ten thousands + 2 hundreds + 4 tens + 9 ones
   B. 50 thousands + 2 hundreds + 40 tens + 9 ones
   C. 5 thousands + 2 hundreds + 40 nines
   D. 50 thousands + 2 hundreds + 40 nines + 9 ones

   4.NBT.2

6. There were 692 cupcakes that needed to be placed into boxes. If each box can hold 5 cupcakes, how many boxes would be needed?

   A. 133
   B. 135
   C. 137
   D. 139

   4.NBT.6

TIP *of the* **DAY**

Tomorrow when you take the assessment, remember key words that tell you to multiply such as product and times. If you see quotient or split evenly, it means to divide.

WEEK 3 : DAY 5

1. What is the remainder when 1385 is divided by 7?

   A. 3
   B. 4
   C. 5
   D. 6

   4.NBT.6

2. What is the product of 3250 and 8?

   A. 24,000
   B. 25,000
   C. 26,000
   D. 27,000

   4.NBT.5

3. There were 17 animals in each exhibit. If there were 58 exhibits, how many animals were there in the zoo?

   A. 776
   B. 896
   C. 986
   D. 1056

   4.NBT.5

4. If Oliver split the 5,400 balloons among 9 schools, how many balloons did each school have?

   A. 60
   B. 600
   C. 70
   D. 700

   4.NBT.6

5. What is 2591 ÷ 3?

   A. 863 r 2
   B. 864 r 1
   C. 864 r 2
   D. 865 r 1

   4.NBT.6

6. What is 7403 times 4?

   A. 28,382
   B. 28,712
   C. 29,542
   D. 29,612

   4.NBT.5

DAY 6
Challenge question

There were 12 bottles of oil in each box and 15 boxes. If the bottles were then moved into smaller boxes that could only hold 9 bottles in a box, how many boxes would be needed?

4.NBT.5
4.NBT.6

28

WEEK 4

Week 4 works with multiplication and division. A multiplication problem is just a number sentence that shows how much larger one number is than another. Key words like "product" or "times" means to multiply and key words like "quotient" means to divide.

You can find detailed video explanations of each problem in the book by visiting:
ArgoPrep.com

1. Which number sentence tells us that the number 84 is 4 times the number 21?

   A. 21 ÷ 4 = 84
   B. 21 × 4 = 84
   C. 21 × 84 = 4
   D. 84 × 4 = 21

   4.OA.1

2. Which statement is represented by 25 × 7 = 175?

   A. The number 175 is 7 times greater than 25.
   B. The number 175 is 7 more than 25.
   C. The number 25 is 7 times greater than 175.
   D. The number 25 is 7 more than 25.

   4.OA.1

3. Which number sentence says that the number 36 is 4 times greater than the number 9?

   A. 36 × 4 = 9
   B. 36 × 9 = 4
   C. 36 = 9 × 4
   D. 36 = 9 + 4

   4.OA.1

4. Which statement is represented by the equation: 12 × 4 = 48?

   A. The number 48 is 12 times larger than the number 4.
   B. The number 48 is 12 more than the number 4.
   C. The number 12 is 4 times larger than the number 48.
   D. The number 12 is 4 more than the number 48.

   4.OA.1

5. Round 3,681,904 to the nearest thousand.

   A. 3,681,900
   B. 3,700,000
   C. 3,680,000
   D. 3,682,000

   4.NBT.3

6. What number goes in the blank to make the sentence true?

   The number 40 is ____ times greater than the number 5.

   A. 6
   B. 7
   C. 8
   D. 9

   4.OA.1

TIP of the DAY

If 6 times 8 equals 48, or 6 × 8 = 48, then 48 is 8 times larger than 6. Forty-eight is also 6 times larger than 8. Remember, a multiplication statement tells us how many times larger one number is than another.

1. Which statement is represented by the equation: $15 \times 9 = 135$?

   A. The number 15 is 9 times larger than 135.
   B. The number 15 is 9 more than 9.
   C. The number 135 is 9 times larger than 15.
   D. The number 135 is 9 more than 15.

   4.OA.1

2. Which equation shows the number that is 8 times larger than 7?

   A. $56 = 7 \times 8$
   B. $15 = 7 + 8$
   C. $7 \times 8 = 72$
   D. $64 = 7 \times 8$

   4.OA.1

3. What number goes in the blank to make the sentence true?

   The number 100 is _____ times greater than the number 10.

   A. 8
   B. 10
   C. 12
   D. 14

   4.OA.1

4. What is the product of 12 and 48?

   A. 60
   B. 496
   C. 576
   D. 636

   4.NBT.5

5. What number is 6 times greater than 12?

   A. 18
   B. 24
   C. 36
   D. 72

   4.OA.1

6. What is the quotient when 1456 is divided by 8?

   A. 180 r 4
   B. 181 r 6
   C. 182
   D. 183 r 2

   4.NBT.6

TIP of the DAY

If you get stuck on a problem, don't focus on what you don't know. Ask yourself what you do know and see if that helps you to begin.

1. There are twice as many tomato plants as there are pepper plants. If there are 18 pepper plants, how many tomato plants are there?

   A. 9
   B. 18
   C. 36
   D. 72

   4.OA.2

2. If Jodi is 5 times as old as Kennedy and Jodi is 30, how old is Kennedy?

   A. 6
   B. 25
   C. 35
   D. 150

   4.OA.2

3. There are 42 white sweaters in the store. This number is 3 times greater than the number of green sweaters. How many green sweaters are there?

   A. 6
   B. 14
   C. 45
   D. 126

   4.OA.2

4. There were 12 cats in the barn and 4 times as many mice. How many mice were there?

   A. 8
   B. 16
   C. 24
   D. 48

   4.OA.2

5. Last week Henry walked 5 times farther than George. If Henry walked 20 miles, how far did George walk?

   A. 4 miles
   B. 25 miles
   C. 75 miles
   D. 100 miles

   4.OA.2

6. Kayla saved 6 times as much money as Joe. If Joe saved $17, how much did Kayla save?

   A. $23
   B. $51
   C. $68
   D. $102

   4.OA.2

TIP of the DAY

You don't have to do the entire problem all at once. Make a plan and then take it one step at a time.

1. Martha baked four times as many pies as Jamie. If Jamie baked 32 pies, how many pies did Martha bake?

   A. 8
   B. 28
   C. 88
   D. 128

   4.OA.2

2. Jimmy's race time was 2 times longer than Johnny's time. If Jimmy's race time was 4 hours, how long was Johnny's race time?

   A. 1 hour   C. 6 hours
   B. 2 hours   D. 8 hours

   4.OA.2

3. Janelle has 9 times as many toys as her brother Dane. If Dane has 18 toys, which equation could be used to find the number of toys Janelle had? Use j to represent Janelle's toys.

   A. $j = 18 \times 9$

   B. $9j = 18$

   C. $j = \dfrac{18}{9}$

   D. $j = 18 + 9$

   4.OA.2

4. Using the chart below, which statement is NOT true?

Person	Age (in years)
Kelli	24
Lee	12
Marley	8
Noah	6

   A. Kelli is three times as old as Marley.
   B. Lee is twice as old as Noah.
   C. Lee is twice as old as Marley.
   D. Kelli is four times as old as Noah.

   4.OA.2

5. Which sentence below is true?

   A. 4 tens + 3 ones > 3 tens + 11 ones

   B. 2 hundreds + 4 tens < two hundred forty

   C. 7 hundreds + 1 ten + 13 ones = seven hundred thirteen

   D. 9 hundreds + 6 ones = 8 hundreds + 16 ones

   4.NBT.2

TIP *of the* **DAY**

When working with word problems, ask yourself some questions. (1) What are the facts? (2) What am I trying to find? (3) Does my answer make sense?

1. Which equation shows that 78 is 3 times as large as 26?

   A. $78 = 26 \times 3$
   B. $26 = 78 \times 3$
   C. $78 = 26 + 3$
   D. $26 = 18 + 3$

   4.OA.1

4. If $27 \times 3 = 81$, then 81 is how many times greater than 3?

   A. 3
   B. 9
   C. 27
   D. 81

   4.OA.1

2. Levi scored 12 goals, which was 3 times more than Sully. How many goals did Sully score?

   A. 3
   B. 4
   C. 9
   D. 15

   4.OA.2

5. If $54 = 9 \times 6$, then fifty-four is nine times as great as _____.

   A. five
   B. six
   C. fifty-four
   D. four hundred eighty-six

   4.OA.1

3. Kara spent 9 times as much as Michelle spent on groceries. If Michelle spent $45 on groceries, how much did Kara spend?

   A. $5
   B. $45
   C. $405
   D. $450

   4.OA.2

6. Fred collected 108 less leaves than Bailey. If Bailey collected 250 leaves, how many leaves did Fred collect?

   A. 42
   B. 142
   C. 258
   D. 358

   4.NBT.4

DAY 6
Challenge question

Julia had $4,048, which is 4 times what Bradley had. How much money did Bradley have?

4.OA.2

34

WEEK 5

This week allows you to exercise what you practiced last week by solving multi-step word problems. You'll work with factors to find numbers that go into other numbers evenly. You will also be asked to find factor pairs.

You can find detailed video explanations of each problem in the book by visiting:
ArgoPrep.com

WEEK 5 : DAY 1

1. Terry wants to buy a $480 bike. He has saved $200 and thinks he can save $40 per month. Which equation shows how many months, *m*, it will take to save enough money to buy the bike?

   A. $m = \dfrac{480 - 200}{40}$

   B. $m = \dfrac{200 - 40}{480}$

   C. $m = (480 - 200) + 40$

   D. $m = \dfrac{480 - 40}{200}$

   4.OA.3

2. Cana is 3 times as old as Josh, who is 2. Eli is 4 years older than Cana. How old is Eli?

   A. 2 years old   C. 6 years old
   B. 3 years old   D. 10 years old

   4.OA.3

3. Violet had 9 shelves that each held 8 dolls. Violet had 4 times as many dolls as Zoey. How many dolls did Zoey have?

   A. 17   C. 68
   B. 18   D. 72

   4.OA.3

4. Steve slept for 8 hours, which was 2 times as long as Tyler slept. Will slept 5 hours longer than Tyler. How many hours did Will sleep?

   A. 4
   B. 5
   C. 8
   D. 9

   4.OA.3

5. Fill in the blank to make the number sentence true: 96 is 6 times greater than _____.

   A. 16
   B. 32
   C. 80
   D. 102

   4.OA.1

6. A red car has 4,186 miles. A blue car has 3,574 miles. A green car has 2 times as many miles as the red and blue cars combined. How many miles are on the green car?

   A. 612   C. 7,760
   B. 1,224   D. 15,520

   4.OA.3

TIP of the DAY

These problems contain more than 1 step. Be sure to carefully complete the first step before moving to the next step.

1. Lara drew 100 greeting cards and handed out 44 to her relatives. If she has 8 friends that she wants to give an even number of cards, how many cards will each friend receive?

   A. 5
   B. 7
   C. 9
   D. 11

   4.OA.3

2. Maggie had 42 nickels, which is 7 times as many as Vika has. Phil has 3 less than Vika. Which equation can be used to find the number of nickels, P, Phil has?

   A. $P = \dfrac{42}{7} - 3$

   B. $P = \dfrac{42 \times 7}{3}$

   C. $P = \dfrac{42}{7} \times 3$

   D. $P = \dfrac{42 - 3}{7}$

   4.OA.3

3. There were 16 necklaces that each had 31 beads. If Shana took all the beads off and put an equal amount on 7 chains, how many beads would be left over?

   A. 0   C. 4
   B. 2   D. 6

   4.OA.3

4. Asa scored 43 points in each of 5 games. If Bill had 26 fewer total points than Asa, how many points did Bill have?

   A. 85
   B. 159
   C. 189
   D. 215

   4.OA.3

5. There was an auditorium that had 35 rows with 25 seats per row. When they remodeled, they got rid of 146 seats and put the seats back so there were only 9 seats in a row. How many rows were there in the auditorium now?

   A. 49
   B. 81
   C. 97
   D. 153

   4.OA.3

6. Ellie ran 5 miles on Monday, Wednesday and Friday. She also ran 8 miles on two other days. Which equation can be used to find the number of miles, m, that Ellie ran?

   A. $m = (8 \times 3) + (2 \times 5)$
   B. $m = 5 \times 3 \times 2 \times 8$
   C. $m = 5 + 3 + 2 + 8$
   D. $m = (5 \times 3) + (2 \times 8)$

   4.OA.3

TIP of the DAY

The review you are doing in this book is going to make you much more prepared for the tests in school. Keep up the good work!

1. Which number is NOT a factor of 24?

   A. 2
   B. 3
   C. 4
   D. 5

   4.OA.4

4. Which number below is composite?

   A. 5
   B. 7
   C. 9
   D. 11

   4.OA.4

2. Which number below is prime?

   A. 25
   B. 53
   C. 70
   D. 99

   4.OA.4

5. What is 496,183 rounded to the nearest ten thousand?

   A. 500,000
   B. 490,000
   C. 496,000
   D. 496,200

   4.NBT.3

3. Most of the factors of 48 are 1, 2, 3, 4, 8, 12, 16, 24 and 48. Which factor is missing?

   A. 5
   B. 6
   C. 7
   D. 9

   4.OA.4

6. Which number has factors that include both 9 and 3?

   A. 12
   B. 15
   C. 18
   D. 21

   4.OA.4

TIP of the DAY

Remember a prime number has EXACTLY 2 factors. (1 is not prime because it has only 1 factor.) Composite numbers have MORE than 2 factors. 9 is composite because its factors are 1, 3, and 9.

WEEK 5 : DAY 4

1. How many factors does 72 have?

   A. 2
   B. 6
   C. 8
   D. 12

   4.OA.4

4. Which number set below has ONLY prime numbers?

   A. 11, 13, 23, 31
   B. 16, 25, 49, 64
   C. 21, 29, 34, 71
   D. 23, 37, 41, 51

   4.OA.4

2. Which number has factors that include 5 and 6?

   A. 11
   B. 15
   C. 30
   D. 54

   4.OA.4

5. What number set contains ALL of the factors of 36?

   A. 1, 2, 3, 4, 9, 12, 16, 18, 36
   B. 1, 2, 3, 4, 6, 9, 12, 18, 36
   C. 1, 2, 3, 4, 6, 8, 12, 16, 18, 36
   D. 1, 2, 3, 4, 9, 12, 18, 36

   4.OA.4

3. Haley bought 3 tops that cost $11 each and 2 pairs of jeans that cost $29 each. She gave the cashier $100. How much change should Haley get?

   A. $3
   B. $5
   C. $7
   D. $9

   4.OA.3

6. Which number is a multiple of 5 and 8?

   A. 13
   B. 20
   C. 48
   D. 80

   4.OA.4

TIP *of the* **DAY**

Tomorrow when you take the assessment, remember to read the questions carefully and think about what is being asked.

ASSESSMENT

1. It took Keith 16 minutes to get home. Then it took him 3 times as long to get ready. How many minutes did it take Keith to get home and get ready?

   A. 16
   B. 48
   C. 64
   D. 80

   4.OA.3

2. Which set of numbers includes ALL of the factors of 39?

   A. 1, 39
   B. 1, 13, 39
   C. 1, 3, 11, 39
   D. 1, 3, 13, 39

   4.OA.4

3. Which set of numbers contains ONLY composite numbers?

   A. 4, 24, 39, 54
   B. 8, 16, 41, 88
   C. 12, 23, 48, 75
   D. 15, 27, 37, 49

   4.OA.4

4. Susan bought a wedding dress that originally cost $454. There was a discount of $76 and then she had to pay $32 for alterations. How much did Susan have to pay for the dress?

   A. $346
   B. $410
   C. $498
   D. $562

   4.OA.3

5. Which number is a multiple of both 7 and 9?

   A. 21
   B. 36
   C. 49
   D. 63

   4.OA.4

6. Which number is a multiple of both 8 and 5?

   A. 16
   B. 24
   C. 35
   D. 40

   4.OA.4

DAY 6

Challenge question

Logan added together all of the prime numbers between 10 and 20. Then he multiplied that sum by the smallest prime number. What number did Logan get?

4.OA.4

WEEK 6

VIDEO EXPLANATIONS ▶ ARGOPREP.COM

Patterns and rules are covered in Week 6. You will be asked to find patterns or make patterns by following certain rules like "add 1" or "subtract 4". You'll also start working with fractions to find equivalent fractions and use models to show what fractions can look like.

You can find detailed video explanations of each problem in the book by visiting:
ArgoPrep.com

1. Sal came up with a rule of "add 4". Two of his numbers were 43 then 47. What would his next number be?

   A. 39
   B. 49
   C. 51
   D. 55

   4.OA.5

2. What is the rule that is shown below?

   A. Subtract 3   C. Add 2
   B. Add 1   D. Add 3

   4.OA.5

3. If the rule is "subtract 2", which of these numbers could be in the pattern 22, 20, 18....?

   A. 6
   B. 5
   C. 3
   D. 1

   4.OA.5

4. The number pattern is "add 3". Which number is after 0, 3, 6?

   A. 5
   B. 7
   C. 8
   D. 9

   4.OA.5

5. Robert listed these numbers: 38, 33, 28, 23, 18. What rule did Robert use?

   A. Subtract 3
   B. Subtract 5
   C. Subtract 8
   D. Subtract 9

   4.OA.5

6. Lucy read for 13 minutes. Micah read 12 times as long as Lucy, and 3 times as long as Rebecca read. Which equation shows how many minutes Rebecca, R, read?

   A. $R = 13 \times 12 \times 3$

   B. $R = \dfrac{13 \times 12}{3}$

   C. $R = 13 \times 12 + 3$

   D. $R = \dfrac{12 \times 3}{13}$

   4.OA.2
   4.OA.3

TIP of the DAY

Rules can be looked at like patterns of shapes. "Add 2" could be shown with 0 triangles, then 2 triangles, then 4 triangles and so on.

1. Ian said he would let his brother Gavin in his room IF Gavin could guess the magic number. Ian said these numbers were in the same pattern as the magic number: 100, 90, 80. Which number could be the magic number?

   A. 40
   B. 55
   C. 63
   D. 72

   4.OA.5

2. Look at the pattern below.

   How many diamonds would be next in the pattern?

   A. 5   C. 3
   B. 4   D. 2

   4.OA.5

3. Find the number that completes this pattern: 19, 28, 37, 46, ___, 64.

   A. 48   C. 62
   B. 55   D. 63

   4.OA.5

4. What number is a multiple of both 3 and 5?

   A. 20
   B. 33
   C. 54
   D. 60

   4.OA.4

5. What rule is shown by the numbers 17, 21, 25, 29?

   A. Add 2
   B. Add 3
   C. Add 4
   D. Add 5

   4.OA.5

6. Start with the number 15 and use the rule "add 2". Which number is NOT in the pattern?

   A. 28
   B. 35
   C. 47
   D. 51

   4.OA.5

TIP of the DAY

Remember in patterns, if the numbers are increasing, the rule is "add". If the numbers are decreasing, the rule is "subtract".

1. Dave drew this fraction:

   Which fraction below is an equivalent fraction to the one Dave drew?

   A.

   B.

   C.

   D.

   4.NF.1

2. What fraction is modeled below?

   A. $\frac{1}{2}$ B. $\frac{1}{3}$ C. $\frac{1}{4}$ D. $\frac{1}{5}$

   4.NF.1

3. There are 8 cookies shown below. Four of them are chocolate. What fraction of the cookies are chocolate?

   A. $\frac{1}{2}$ B. $\frac{1}{3}$ C. $\frac{1}{4}$ D. $\frac{1}{8}$

   4.NF.1

4. Which model is shaded to represent a fraction equivalent to $\frac{1}{4}$?

   A.   C.

   B.   D.

   4.NF.1

5. What fraction does the model below represent?

   A. $\frac{1}{2}$ B. $\frac{2}{3}$ C. $\frac{2}{4}$ D. $\frac{2}{5}$

   4.NF.1

6. Which statement below is true?

   A. 4,000 + 500 + 7 = 457
   B. 3 tens + 14 ones > 30 ones
   C. 8 hundreds + 6 tens > 9 hundreds
   D. 972 > 9 hundreds + 8 tens

   4.NBT.2

TIP of the DAY

Try to remember, fractions are just *part* of a whole number. If your juice glass is half-full, that is a fraction, $\frac{1}{2}$. If it is 9:15, it is one-quarter of an hour past 9.

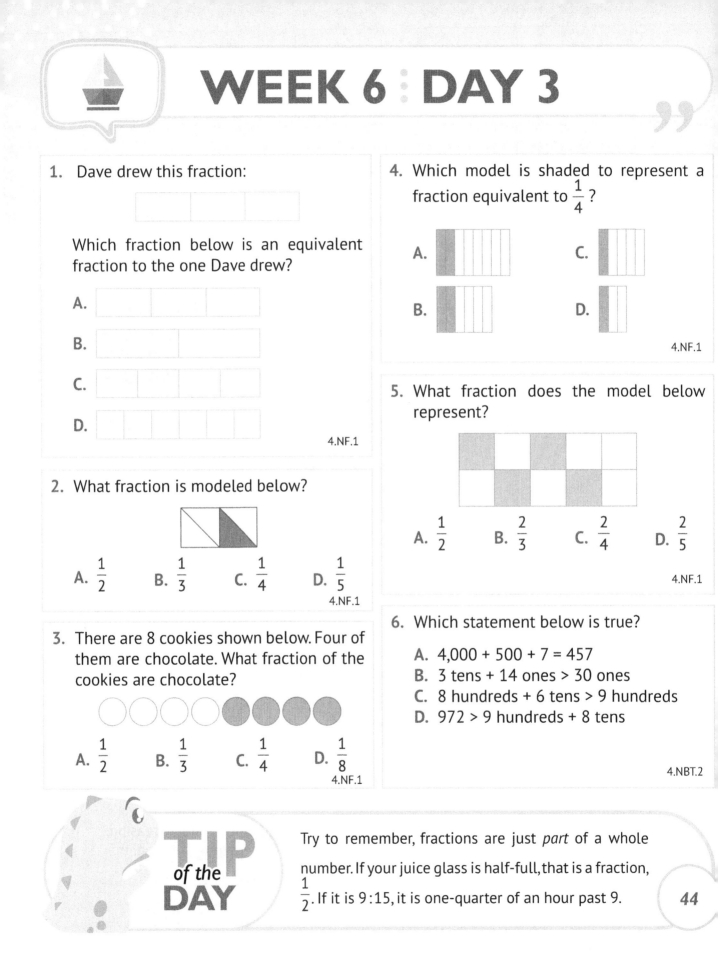

1. Alice shaded the 2 same-sized models below to represent $\frac{1}{2}$ and $\frac{3}{6}$.

   She believes that $\frac{1}{2}$ is equivalent to $\frac{3}{6}$. Is Alice correct or incorrect and why?

   A. She is correct because multiplying the numerator and denominator in $\frac{1}{2}$ by the same number equals $\frac{3}{6}$.

   B. She is correct because adding 2 to the numerator and denominator of $\frac{1}{2}$ equals $\frac{3}{6}$.

   C. She is incorrect because $\frac{1}{2} + \frac{1}{2}$ does not equal $\frac{3}{6}$.

   D. She is incorrect because the numerators and denominators are not the same.

   4.NF.1

2. The car only went $\frac{6}{8}$ down the road. Which model below shows how far the car went down the road?

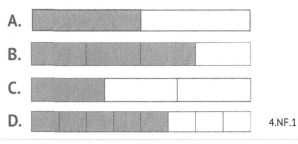

   A.

   B.

   C.

   D.

   4.NF.1

3. Reginald deposited $1259 into his bank account last week. This week he withdrew $482 and $99. How much does he have left in his account?

   A. $1840   C. $876

   B. $1642   D. $678   4.OA.3

4. Look at the drawing below.   4.NF.1

   Which of the following fractions is equivalent to the above drawing?

   A. $\frac{1}{2}$ B. $\frac{1}{3}$ C. $\frac{1}{4}$ D. $\frac{2}{5}$

5. Which model below represents a fraction equivalent to $\frac{1}{3}$?

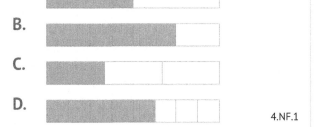

   A.

   B.

   C.

   D.   4.NF.1

6. There are 24 hours in a day. If Fluffy the Cat spent 12 hours sleeping, which of the following fractions is NOT equivalent to the amount of time Fluffy spent sleeping?

   4.NF.1

   A. $\frac{6}{10}$ B. $\frac{6}{12}$ C. $\frac{4}{8}$ D. $\frac{1}{2}$

ASSESSMENT

1. Which set of numbers has the rule "subtract 3"?

   A. 14, 17, 21, 24
   B. 43, 39, 35, 31
   C. 57, 54, 51, 48
   D. 35, 30, 25, 20

   4.OA.5

2. Look at the model below.

   Which of the following fractions is equivalent to the model above?

   A. $\frac{1}{3}$ B. $\frac{2}{4}$ C. $\frac{2}{3}$ D. $\frac{4}{5}$

   4.NF.1

3. What pattern is shown below?

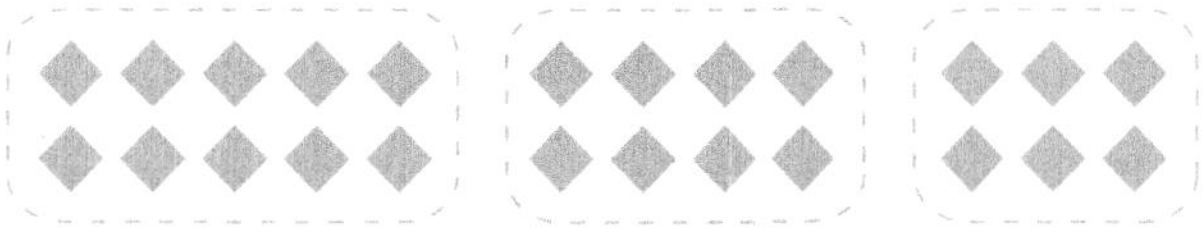

   A. + 2   C. −1
   B. + 1   D. −2

   4.OA.5

4. Which model below represents $\frac{4}{5}$?

   A. 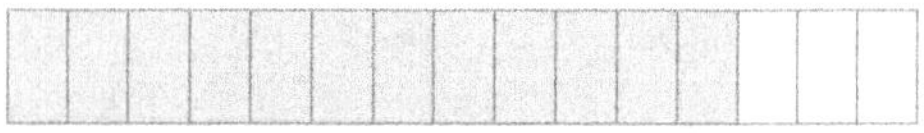
   B.
   C.
   D.

   4.NF.1

5. If 63 = 9 × 7, then sixty-three is seven times as great as _____.

   A. six
   B. nine
   C. sixty-three
   D. four hundred forty-one

   4.OA.1

6. Find the next number in this pattern: 91, _____, 81, 76, 71, 66...

   A. 86
   B. 84
   C. 82
   D. 80

   4.OA.5

DAY 6

Challenge question

Look at the pattern below.

99 88 77 66 55 44 33

What is the next object in the pattern?   4.OA.5

ARGOPREP.COM

: **VIDEO**
EXPLANATIONS ▶

73.05

Comparisons are some of what you'll practice in Week 7. You'll have a chance to use the comparison symbols (<, >, =) to make true number sentences that involve fractions and compare them to benchmark fractions like $\frac{1}{4}$, $\frac{1}{2}$ and $\frac{3}{4}$.

You can find detailed video explanations of each problem in the book by visiting:
ArgoPrep.com

1. Which number sentence below is true?

   A. $\frac{4}{5} < \frac{3}{4}$

   B. $\frac{4}{5} = \frac{3}{4}$

   C. $\frac{3}{4} < \frac{4}{5}$

   D. $\frac{3}{4} > \frac{4}{5}$

   4.NF.2

2. Greg drank $\frac{1}{2}$ of his milk and Riley drank $\frac{1}{3}$ of hers. Which statement is true?

   A. $\frac{1}{2} > \frac{1}{3}$

   B. $\frac{1}{3} > \frac{1}{2}$

   C. $\frac{1}{2} = \frac{1}{3}$

   D. $\frac{1}{2} < \frac{1}{3}$

   4.NF.2

3. Looking at the models below, which statement is true?

   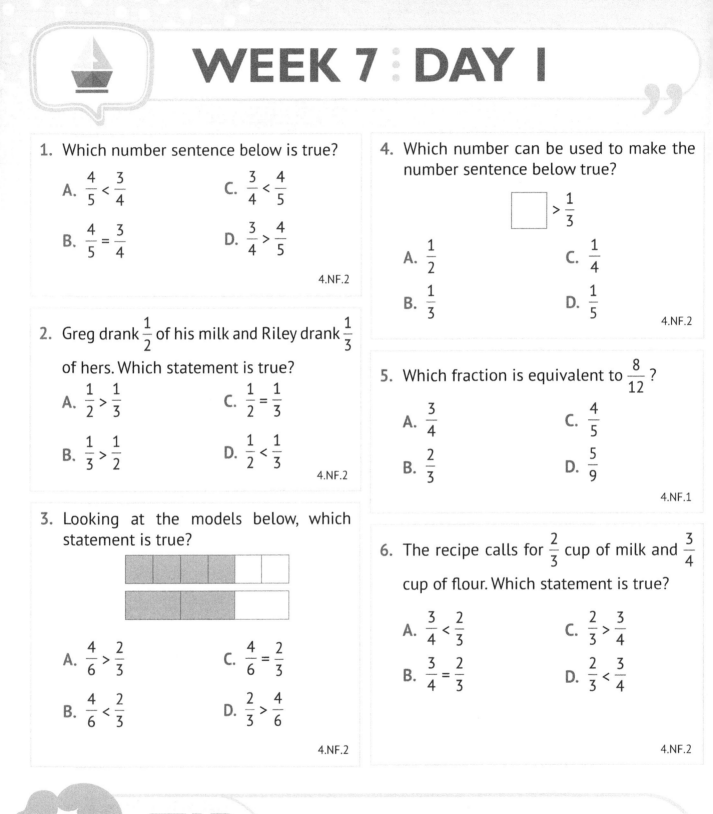

   A. $\frac{4}{6} > \frac{2}{3}$

   B. $\frac{4}{6} < \frac{2}{3}$

   C. $\frac{4}{6} = \frac{2}{3}$

   D. $\frac{2}{3} > \frac{4}{6}$

   4.NF.2

4. Which number can be used to make the number sentence below true?

   $$\boxed{} > \frac{1}{3}$$

   A. $\frac{1}{2}$

   B. $\frac{1}{3}$

   C. $\frac{1}{4}$

   D. $\frac{1}{5}$

   4.NF.2

5. Which fraction is equivalent to $\frac{8}{12}$?

   A. $\frac{3}{4}$

   B. $\frac{2}{3}$

   C. $\frac{4}{5}$

   D. $\frac{5}{9}$

   4.NF.1

6. The recipe calls for $\frac{2}{3}$ cup of milk and $\frac{3}{4}$ cup of flour. Which statement is true?

   A. $\frac{3}{4} < \frac{2}{3}$

   B. $\frac{3}{4} = \frac{2}{3}$

   C. $\frac{2}{3} > \frac{3}{4}$

   D. $\frac{2}{3} < \frac{3}{4}$

   4.NF.2

TIP of the DAY

Remember: To accurately compare fractions, they must have the same denominator.

48

1. Which number sentence is true?

   A. $\dfrac{7}{8} > \dfrac{6}{8}$

   B. $\dfrac{7}{8} = \dfrac{6}{8}$

   C. $\dfrac{6}{8} > \dfrac{7}{8}$

   D. $\dfrac{7}{8} < \dfrac{6}{8}$

   4.NF.2

2. Find the fraction that makes the number sentence true.

   $$\dfrac{3}{4} = \boxed{}$$

   A. $\dfrac{8}{10}$

   B. $\dfrac{6}{8}$

   C. $\dfrac{4}{5}$

   D. $\dfrac{4}{6}$

   4.NF.2

3. Carly ran $\dfrac{3}{12}$ of a mile and Jorge ran $\dfrac{1}{3}$. Which number sentence is true?

   A. $\dfrac{3}{12} = \dfrac{1}{3}$

   B. $\dfrac{3}{12} > \dfrac{1}{3}$

   C. $\dfrac{1}{3} < \dfrac{3}{12}$

   D. $\dfrac{1}{3} > \dfrac{3}{12}$

   4.NF.2

4. Jackson added $\dfrac{1}{5}$ cup of tea to $\dfrac{1}{3}$ cup of water. Which number sentence is true?

   A. $\dfrac{1}{5} < \dfrac{1}{3}$

   B. $\dfrac{1}{5} = \dfrac{1}{3}$

   C. $\dfrac{1}{3} < \dfrac{1}{5}$

   D. $\dfrac{1}{5} > \dfrac{1}{3}$

   4.NF.2

5. Using the models below, which number sentence is true?

   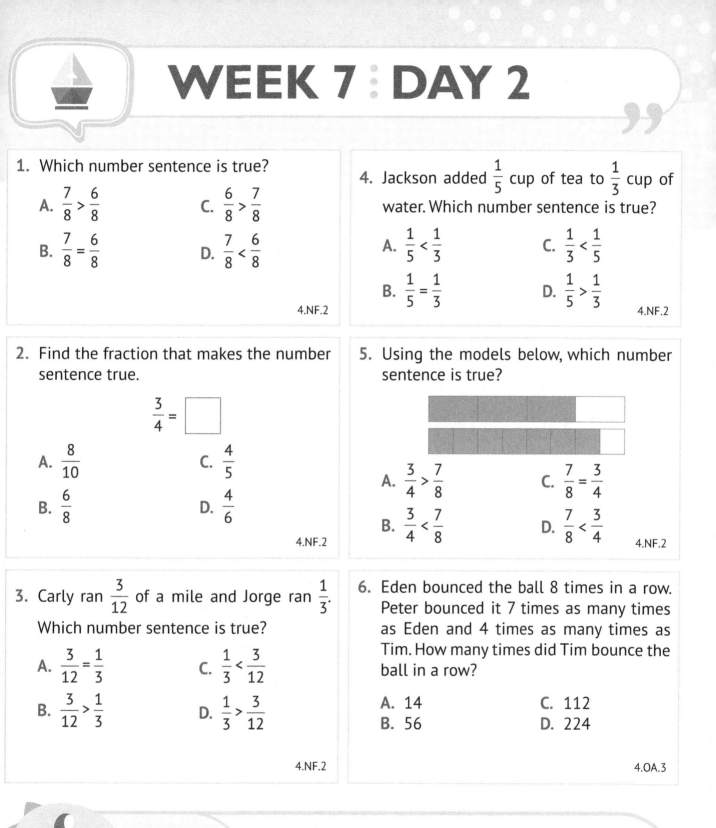

   A. $\dfrac{3}{4} > \dfrac{7}{8}$

   B. $\dfrac{3}{4} < \dfrac{7}{8}$

   C. $\dfrac{7}{8} = \dfrac{3}{4}$

   D. $\dfrac{7}{8} < \dfrac{3}{4}$

   4.NF.2

6. Eden bounced the ball 8 times in a row. Peter bounced it 7 times as many times as Eden and 4 times as many times as Tim. How many times did Tim bounce the ball in a row?

   A. 14

   B. 56

   C. 112

   D. 224

   4.OA.3

TIP of the DAY

Let fractions be your friends - can you think of any time throughout a day that you use fractions? (Time, distance, baking/cooking, running, etc.)

1. Which number sentence is true?

   A. $\dfrac{9}{15} > \dfrac{3}{5}$

   B. $\dfrac{9}{15} < \dfrac{3}{5}$

   C. $\dfrac{3}{5} = \dfrac{9}{15}$

   D. $\dfrac{3}{5} > \dfrac{9}{15}$

   4.NF.2

2. Mrs. Pate walked $\dfrac{7}{8}$ of a kilometer and Mr. Pate walked $\dfrac{3}{4}$ of a kilometer. Which number sentence is true?

   A. $\dfrac{7}{8} = \dfrac{3}{4}$

   B. $\dfrac{7}{8} > \dfrac{3}{4}$

   C. $\dfrac{7}{8} < \dfrac{3}{4}$

   D. $\dfrac{3}{4} > \dfrac{7}{8}$

   4.NF.2

3. Which number sentence is true?

   A. $\dfrac{3}{8} = \dfrac{1}{4}$

   B. $\dfrac{3}{8} < \dfrac{1}{4}$

   C. $\dfrac{1}{4} > \dfrac{3}{8}$

   D. $\dfrac{1}{4} < \dfrac{3}{8}$

   4.NF.2

4. Which number set below has ONLY numbers that are composite?

   A. $5, 9, 14, 19$
   B. $6, 10, 13, 18$
   C. $7, 11, 19, 23$
   D. $8, 12, 21, 25$

   4.OA.4

5. Which fraction would make the number sentence true?

   $$\dfrac{2}{5} > \boxed{}$$

   A. $\dfrac{1}{3}$

   B. $\dfrac{2}{4}$

   C. $\dfrac{3}{5}$

   D. $\dfrac{4}{6}$

   4.NF.2

6. Ricky and Becky colored the same amount of their papers. Ricky colored $\dfrac{1}{2}$ of his paper. Which number sentence is NOT true?

   A. $\dfrac{1}{2} = \dfrac{6}{12}$

   B. $\dfrac{1}{2} = \dfrac{8}{14}$

   C. $\dfrac{1}{2} = \dfrac{5}{10}$

   D. $\dfrac{1}{2} = \dfrac{4}{8}$

   4.NF.2

TIP of the DAY

If you can't figure out which fraction is larger, draw your own model and see if that makes the answer clearer.

1. Donald ate $\frac{1}{2}$ of a pizza and Ronald ate $\frac{5}{8}$ of a pizza. Which number sentence is true?

   A. $\frac{5}{8} < \frac{1}{2}$ C. $\frac{1}{2} > \frac{5}{8}$

   B. $\frac{5}{8} > \frac{1}{2}$ D. $\frac{1}{2} = \frac{5}{8}$

   4.NF.2

2. Which number sentence is true?

   A. $\frac{3}{6} < \frac{1}{2}$ C. $\frac{1}{2} = \frac{3}{6}$

   B. $\frac{3}{6} > \frac{1}{2}$ D. $\frac{1}{2} > \frac{3}{6}$

   4.NF.2

3. Which fraction makes the number sentence true?

   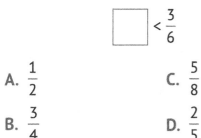

   $\boxed{} < \frac{3}{6}$

   A. $\frac{1}{2}$ C. $\frac{5}{8}$

   B. $\frac{3}{4}$ D. $\frac{2}{5}$

   4.NF.2

4. The Hoard family has completed $\frac{2}{3}$ of their trip and the Bards have completed $\frac{5}{6}$ of their trip. Which number sentence is true?

   A. $\frac{5}{6} < \frac{2}{3}$ C. $\frac{2}{3} < \frac{5}{6}$

   B. $\frac{5}{6} = \frac{2}{3}$ D. $\frac{2}{3} > \frac{5}{6}$

   4.NF.2

5. Which set of numbers has ALL of the factors of 42?

   A. 1, 2, 3, 6, 7, 14, 21, 42
   B. 1, 2, 4, 6, 7, 8, 21, 42
   C. 1, 2, 3, 4, 6, 7, 8, 21, 42
   D. 1, 2, 3, 4, 6, 7, 8, 14, 21, 42

   4.OA.4

6. Looking at the models below, which number sentence is true?

   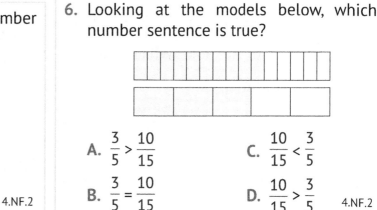

   A. $\frac{3}{5} > \frac{10}{15}$ C. $\frac{10}{15} < \frac{3}{5}$

   B. $\frac{3}{5} = \frac{10}{15}$ D. $\frac{10}{15} > \frac{3}{5}$

   4.NF.2

TIP of the DAY

Fractions are used everyday, both in and out of the classroom so be sure to study these types of problems.

WEEK 7 : DAY 5

1. Which number sentence is true?

    A. $\dfrac{3}{4} > \dfrac{7}{8}$ C. $\dfrac{7}{8} > \dfrac{3}{4}$

    B. $\dfrac{3}{4} = \dfrac{7}{8}$ D. $\dfrac{7}{8} < \dfrac{3}{4}$

    4.NF.2

2. What fraction completes the number sentence to make it true?

    $$\boxed{} = \dfrac{1}{3}$$

    A. $\dfrac{1}{5}$ C. $\dfrac{3}{8}$

    B. $\dfrac{1}{2}$ D. $\dfrac{2}{6}$

    4.NF.2

3. Steve drove for $\dfrac{4}{5}$ of an hour and Traci drove for $\dfrac{7}{8}$ of an hour. Which number sentence is true?

    A. $\dfrac{4}{5} > \dfrac{7}{8}$ C. $\dfrac{7}{8} = \dfrac{4}{5}$

    B. $\dfrac{4}{5} < \dfrac{7}{8}$ D. $\dfrac{7}{8} < \dfrac{4}{5}$

    4.NF.2

4. Use the models below to find the number sentence that is true.

    A. $\dfrac{3}{6} > \dfrac{1}{2}$ C. $\dfrac{1}{2} > \dfrac{3}{6}$

    B. $\dfrac{3}{6} < \dfrac{1}{2}$ D. $\dfrac{1}{2} = \dfrac{3}{6}$

    4.NF.2

5. One-fourth of the candle burned on Monday and two-fifths on Tuesday. Which number sentence is true?

    A. $\dfrac{2}{5} < \dfrac{1}{4}$ C. $\dfrac{1}{4} > \dfrac{2}{5}$

    B. $\dfrac{2}{5} = \dfrac{1}{4}$ D. $\dfrac{1}{4} < \dfrac{2}{5}$

    4.NF.2

6. What is 1223 divided by 4?

    A. 30 r 3
    B. 35 r 3
    C. 305 r 3
    D. 3005 r 3

    4.NBT.6

DAY 6
Challenge question

Draw a model that proves $\dfrac{3}{4}$ is equal to $\dfrac{6}{8}$.

4.NF.2

WEEK 8

Week 8 allows you to work with the addition and subtraction of like fractions, fractions that have the same denominator. It will build on what you practiced last week by offering chances to work with equivalent fractions and mixed numbers.

You can find detailed video explanations of each problem in the book by visiting: ArgoPrep.com

WEEK 8 : DAY 1

1. What is $\frac{1}{5}$ added to $\frac{3}{4}$?

   A. $\frac{4}{9}$ C. $\frac{4}{20}$

   B. $\frac{7}{10}$ D. $\frac{19}{20}$

4.NF.3

2. Find: $\frac{5}{8} - \frac{1}{4}$.

   A. $\frac{4}{4}$ C. $\frac{3}{8}$

   B. $\frac{1}{4}$ D. $\frac{4}{8}$

4.NF.3

3. What does $\frac{1}{3} + \frac{1}{4}$ equal?

   A. $\frac{7}{12}$ C. $\frac{2}{12}$

   B. $\frac{2}{5}$ D. $\frac{2}{7}$

4.NF.3

4. $\frac{9}{12} - \frac{3}{8} = ?$

   A. $\frac{6}{4}$ C. $\frac{3}{4}$

   B. $\frac{3}{8}$ D. $\frac{5}{12}$

4.NF.3

5. Find the difference between $\frac{5}{6}$ and $\frac{2}{5}$.

   A. $\frac{1}{2}$ C. $\frac{3}{1}$

   B. $\frac{13}{30}$ D. $\frac{3}{10}$

4.NF.3

6. What is the sum of $\frac{1}{8}$, $\frac{1}{4}$ and $\frac{1}{3}$?

   A. $\frac{17}{24}$ C. $\frac{3}{24}$

   B. $\frac{3}{15}$ D. $\frac{15}{24}$

4.NF.3

TIP of the DAY

Don't forget that if you want to add or subtract fractions or mixed numbers, they need to have the same denominator.

WEEK 8 : DAY 2

1. What addition statement is represented by the model below?

A. $\frac{3}{15}+\frac{5}{15}+\frac{3}{15}=\frac{11}{15}$

C. $\frac{2}{15}+\frac{4}{15}+\frac{3}{15}=\frac{9}{15}$

B. $\frac{2}{15}+\frac{5}{15}+\frac{3}{15}=\frac{10}{15}$

D. $\frac{2}{15}+\frac{5}{15}+\frac{4}{15}=\frac{11}{15}$

4.NF.3

2. Which equation below is true?

A. $\frac{5}{7}-\frac{2}{7}+\frac{3}{7}=\frac{7}{7}$

C. $\frac{6}{7}-\frac{1}{7}+\frac{3}{7}=\frac{7}{7}$

B. $\frac{6}{7}-\frac{2}{7}+\frac{4}{7}=\frac{7}{7}$

D. $\frac{6}{7}-\frac{2}{7}+\frac{3}{7}=\frac{7}{7}$

4.NF.3

3. What is another way to write $\frac{10}{9}$?

A. $\frac{3}{9}+\frac{4}{9}+\frac{3}{9}$

C. $\frac{5}{9}+\frac{2}{9}+\frac{4}{9}$

B. $\frac{3}{9}+\frac{1}{9}+\frac{2}{9}$

D. $\frac{2}{9}+\frac{5}{9}+\frac{4}{9}$

4.NF.3

4. Randy went to the store and bought 6 dozen eggs for $2/dozen. He also bought 5 gallons of milk for $4/gallon. He paid with 2 twenty-dollar bills. How much change did he get?

A. $8
B. $10
C. $12
D. $14

4.OA.3

5. Which number sentence below is true?

A. $\frac{9}{7}+\frac{2}{7}-\frac{1}{7}=\frac{8}{7}$

C. $\frac{4}{11}+\frac{2}{11}+\frac{1}{11}=\frac{8}{11}$

B. $\frac{8}{4}-\frac{2}{4}+\frac{1}{4}=\frac{7}{4}$

D. $\frac{6}{8}-\frac{2}{8}+\frac{1}{8}=\frac{6}{8}$

4.NF.3

6. What is another way to write $\frac{13}{11}$?

A. $\frac{9}{11}-\frac{3}{11}+\frac{5}{11}$

C. $\frac{4}{11}+\frac{6}{11}+\frac{3}{11}$

B. $\frac{8}{11}-\frac{2}{11}+\frac{5}{11}$

D. $\frac{5}{11}+\frac{7}{11}+\frac{2}{11}$

4.NF.3

TIP of the DAY

When adding fractions that have the same denominators, keep that denominator and add the numerators together.

55

1. What is $5\frac{1}{3} + 2\frac{2}{3}$?

   A. $7\frac{2}{3}$ C. $8\frac{1}{3}$

   B. 8 D. $8\frac{2}{3}$

4.NF.3

2. Find: $10\frac{1}{8} - 7\frac{2}{8}$.

   A. $3\frac{1}{8}$ C. $2\frac{1}{8}$

   B. 3 D. $2\frac{7}{8}$

4.NF.3

3. What is the sum of $12\frac{4}{6} + 4\frac{1}{6}$?

   A. $8\frac{3}{6}$ C. $16\frac{5}{6}$

   B. $16\frac{3}{6}$ D. 17

4.NF.3

4. What is the difference between $13\frac{4}{6}$ and $7\frac{2}{6}$?

   A. $6\frac{2}{6}$ C. $6\frac{6}{6}$

   B. $6\frac{4}{6}$ D. $7\frac{2}{6}$

4.NF.3

5. In the number 144,698, how many times greater is the 4 in the ten thousands place than the 4 in the thousands place?

   A. 1
   B. 10
   C. 100
   D. 1,000

4.NBT.1

6. What is $15\frac{5}{8} + 18\frac{7}{8}$?

   A. $3\frac{2}{8}$ C. $34\frac{4}{8}$

   B. $33\frac{7}{8}$ D. $34\frac{7}{8}$

4.NF.3

TIP of the DAY

If you have to "borrow" a one to subtract fractions, don't forget to add that one as an equivalent fraction to the original fraction.

WEEK 8 : DAY 4

1. Lulu used $4\frac{1}{8}$ pounds of soil for her garden on Wednesday. On Thursday she used $6\frac{4}{8}$ pounds of soil. How many pounds of soil did Lulu use altogether?

   A. $11\frac{1}{8}$

   B. $10\frac{5}{8}$

   C. $10\frac{3}{8}$

   D. $2\frac{3}{8}$

   4.NF.3

2. Jenny's race time was $2\frac{4}{5}$ hours and Matt raced for $3\frac{1}{5}$ hours. What was their combined times?

   A. $1\frac{3}{5}$ hours

   B. $4\frac{4}{5}$ hours

   C. 6 hours

   D. $6\frac{2}{5}$ hours

   4.NF.3

3. Sam and Brendon were trying to lose weight for wrestling. Sam lost $\frac{7}{8}$ of a pound and Brendon lost 2 pounds. How many pounds more did Brendon lose?

   A. $2\frac{7}{8}$

   B. $1\frac{7}{8}$

   C. $1\frac{1}{8}$

   D. $\frac{7}{8}$

   4.NF.3

4. Lisa swam her race in $4\frac{1}{6}$ minutes. Scott took $3\frac{4}{6}$ minutes. How much faster was Scott?

   A. $7\frac{5}{6}$ minutes

   B. $1\frac{3}{6}$ minutes

   C. $1\frac{1}{6}$ minutes

   D. $\frac{3}{6}$ of a minute

   4.NF.3

5. Using the model below, which number sentence is true?

   A. $\frac{10}{15} > \frac{3}{5}$

   B. $\frac{10}{15} < \frac{3}{5}$

   C. $\frac{3}{5} = \frac{10}{15}$

   D. $\frac{3}{5} > \frac{10}{15}$

   4.NF.2

TIP of the DAY

When trying to answer word problems, remember to list the facts first, and then determine what the question is asking. Check your answer to make sure it is reasonable.

57

1. Which number sentence is true?

   A. $\dfrac{1}{4} > \dfrac{2}{5}$

   B. $\dfrac{7}{8} > \dfrac{8}{9}$

   C. $\dfrac{3}{4} < \dfrac{6}{8}$

   D. $\dfrac{12}{15} = \dfrac{4}{5}$

   4.NF.2

2. Sugar Shack sells sugar in $50\dfrac{1}{4}$ pound bags. Super Sugar sells it in $45\dfrac{3}{4}$ pound bags. What is the difference between the 2 bags?

   A. $3\dfrac{2}{4}$ pounds

   B. $4\dfrac{2}{4}$ pounds

   C. $5\dfrac{2}{4}$ pounds

   D. 6 pounds

   4.NF.3

3. What is $25\dfrac{7}{8} - 20$?

   A. $4\dfrac{7}{8}$

   B. $5\dfrac{1}{8}$

   C. $5\dfrac{7}{8}$

   D. $6\dfrac{1}{8}$

   4.NF.3

4. Which statement is true?

   A. $\dfrac{1}{9} + \dfrac{5}{9} - \dfrac{3}{9} = \dfrac{3}{9}$

   B. $\dfrac{2}{8} - \dfrac{1}{8} + \dfrac{4}{8} = \dfrac{6}{8}$

   C. $\dfrac{4}{10} + \dfrac{7}{10} - \dfrac{2}{10} = \dfrac{10}{12}$

   D. $\dfrac{8}{12} - \dfrac{5}{12} + \dfrac{4}{12} = \dfrac{8}{12}$

   4.NF.3

5. Suzanne bought $10\dfrac{3}{5}$ pounds of strawberries and Kim bought $8\dfrac{4}{5}$ pounds. How many pounds of strawberries did they buy altogether?

   A. $1\dfrac{4}{5}$

   B. $2\dfrac{1}{5}$

   C. $18\dfrac{2}{5}$

   D. $19\dfrac{2}{5}$

   4.NF.3

6. Find the sum of $\dfrac{3}{8}, \dfrac{5}{12}$ and $\dfrac{1}{4}$.

   A. $\dfrac{9}{12}$

   B. $\dfrac{9}{24}$

   C. $\dfrac{24}{24}$

   D. $\dfrac{25}{24}$

   4.NF.3

DAY 6
Challenge question

Erik bought $3\dfrac{1}{8}$ pounds of peanuts. At the party $2\dfrac{2}{8}$ pounds were eaten so he bought 4 pounds more. How many pounds of peanuts does Erik have now?

4.NF.3

WEEK 9

: VIDEO
EXPLANATIONS ► ARGOPREP.COM

This week, fractions are being multiplied by whole numbers. You will begin to see how fractions are used in the real world and how they apply to word problems.

You can find detailed video explanations of each problem in the book by visiting:
ArgoPrep.com

1. The fraction model represents 5 whole units.

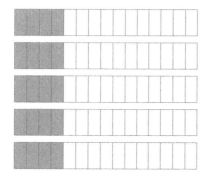

Which number sentence represents the amount of the fraction model that is shaded?

A. $5 \times \dfrac{4}{15} = \dfrac{20}{15}$

C. $5 \times \dfrac{1}{15} = \dfrac{5}{15}$

B. $4 \times \dfrac{1}{15} = \dfrac{4}{15}$

D. $15 \times \dfrac{1}{4} = \dfrac{15}{4}$

4.NF.4

2. $7 \times \dfrac{1}{8} = ?$

A. $\dfrac{7}{56}$

C. $\dfrac{7}{8}$

B. $\dfrac{7}{15}$

D. $\dfrac{8}{7}$

4.NF.4

3. It takes Maria $\dfrac{4}{5}$ of an hour to clean her room. Which expression represents the amount of time it would take Maria to clean her room 3 times?

A. $4 \times \dfrac{3}{5}$

C. $3 \times \dfrac{1}{5}$

B. $3 \times \dfrac{4}{5}$

D. $4 \times \dfrac{1}{5}$

4.NF.4

4. If there was $\dfrac{1}{7}$ of a gallon of lemonade left in each carton, how many gallons are left in 12 cartons?

A. $\dfrac{7}{12}$

C. $\dfrac{12}{5}$

B. $\dfrac{5}{12}$

D. $\dfrac{12}{7}$

4.NF.4

5. Sofia swam for $\dfrac{1}{2}$ of an hour on 3 different days. Which model shows the amount of time Sofia swam?

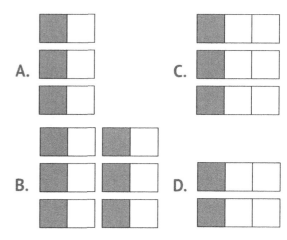

4.NF.4

1. Juan ran $\frac{1}{3}$ mile each day for 4 days. How many miles did Juan run?

   A. $\frac{3}{4}$

   B. $\frac{4}{3}$

   C. $1\frac{3}{4}$

   D. $4\frac{1}{3}$

   4.NF.4

2. Which number sentence is true?

   A. $\frac{1}{3} > \frac{4}{5}$

   B. $\frac{8}{8} > \frac{1}{2}$

   C. $\frac{9}{10} < \frac{3}{5}$

   D. $\frac{5}{6} < \frac{2}{3}$

   4.NF.2

3. Rudy worked on his homework for $\frac{3}{4}$ of an hour per day for 6 days. Which expression can be used to find the number of hours Rudy spent on homework?

   A. $\frac{3}{4} \times 6 = ?$

   B. $\frac{3}{4} \times \frac{1}{6} = ?$

   C. $6 \times \frac{1}{4} = ?$

   D. $6 \times \frac{1}{6} = ?$

   4.NF.4

4. Look at the model below. Which scenario could it be describing?

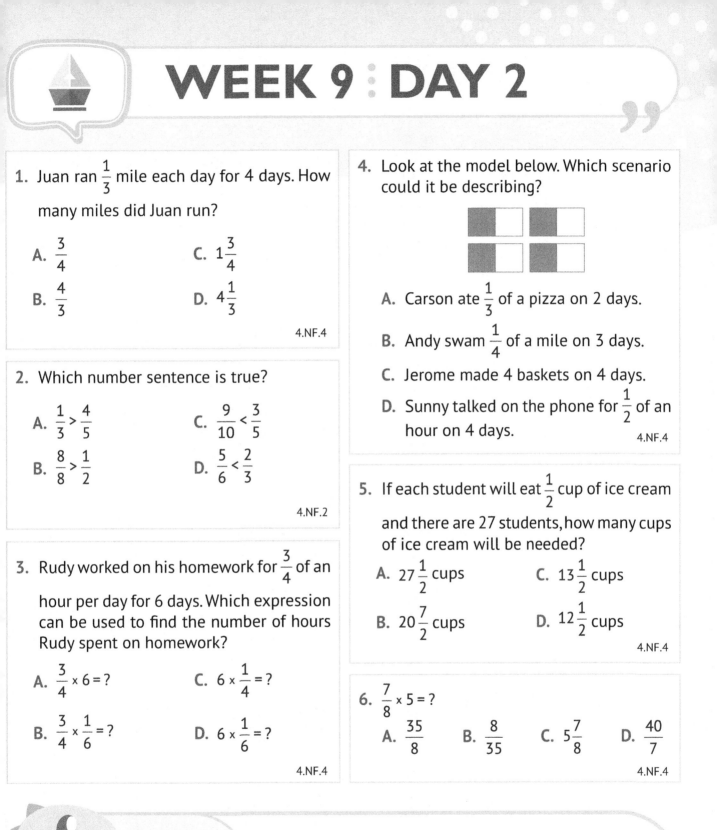

   A. Carson ate $\frac{1}{3}$ of a pizza on 2 days.

   B. Andy swam $\frac{1}{4}$ of a mile on 3 days.

   C. Jerome made 4 baskets on 4 days.

   D. Sunny talked on the phone for $\frac{1}{2}$ of an hour on 4 days.

   4.NF.4

5. If each student will eat $\frac{1}{2}$ cup of ice cream and there are 27 students, how many cups of ice cream will be needed?

   A. $27\frac{1}{2}$ cups

   B. $20\frac{7}{2}$ cups

   C. $13\frac{1}{2}$ cups

   D. $12\frac{1}{2}$ cups

   4.NF.4

6. $\frac{7}{8} \times 5 = ?$

   A. $\frac{35}{8}$

   B. $\frac{8}{35}$

   C. $5\frac{7}{8}$

   D. $\frac{40}{7}$

   4.NF.4

1. If Mrs. Johnson uses $\frac{2}{3}$ of a loaf of bread per day for her family's lunches, how many loaves of bread do they use per week (5 days)?

A. $5\frac{2}{3}$

C. $\frac{10}{3}$

B. $\frac{15}{2}$

D. $\frac{5}{3}$

4.NF.4

2. Which number sentence is modeled below?

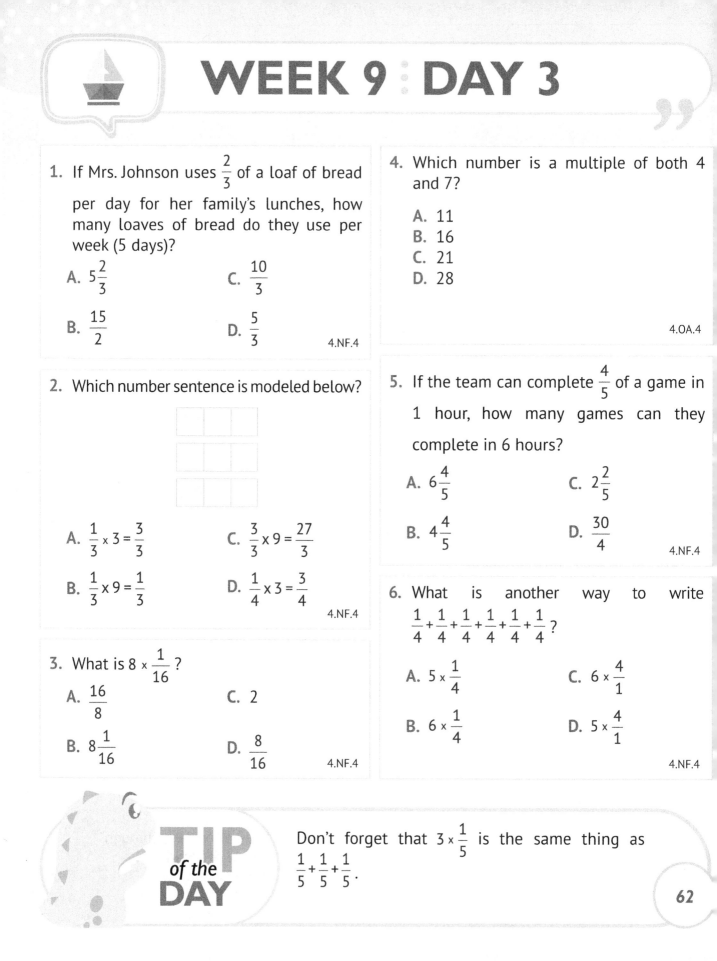

A. $\frac{1}{3} \times 3 = \frac{3}{3}$

C. $\frac{3}{3} \times 9 = \frac{27}{3}$

B. $\frac{1}{3} \times 9 = \frac{1}{3}$

D. $\frac{1}{4} \times 3 = \frac{3}{4}$

4.NF.4

3. What is $8 \times \frac{1}{16}$?

A. $\frac{16}{8}$

C. 2

B. $8\frac{1}{16}$

D. $\frac{8}{16}$

4.NF.4

4. Which number is a multiple of both 4 and 7?

A. 11
B. 16
C. 21
D. 28

4.OA.4

5. If the team can complete $\frac{4}{5}$ of a game in 1 hour, how many games can they complete in 6 hours?

A. $6\frac{4}{5}$

C. $2\frac{2}{5}$

B. $4\frac{4}{5}$

D. $\frac{30}{4}$

4.NF.4

6. What is another way to write $\frac{1}{4} + \frac{1}{4} + \frac{1}{4} + \frac{1}{4} + \frac{1}{4} + \frac{1}{4}$?

A. $5 \times \frac{1}{4}$

C. $6 \times \frac{4}{1}$

B. $6 \times \frac{1}{4}$

D. $5 \times \frac{4}{1}$

4.NF.4

TIP of the DAY

Don't forget that $3 \times \frac{1}{5}$ is the same thing as $\frac{1}{5} + \frac{1}{5} + \frac{1}{5}$.

1. What scenario could be represented by the model below?

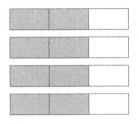

A. Josh ran $\frac{8}{3}$ of a mile on 4 days.

B. Harry ate $\frac{2}{3}$ of a pizza for 4 days.

C. Chelsea had 8 pieces of pie over 4 days.

D. Halle walked $\frac{1}{3}$ of a mile on 8 days.

4.NF.4

2. Jo goes to the Farmer's Market. The prices are shown below.

Item	Cost
Apples	$9
Bananas	$12
Carrots	$7

How much does Jo spend if she buys 8 bags of apples, 10 bunches of bananas and 5 bundles of carrots?

A. $215
B. $218
C. $220
D. $227

4.OA.3

3. What is **NOT** another way to write $\frac{1}{3}+\frac{1}{3}+\frac{1}{3}+\frac{1}{3}+\frac{1}{3}+\frac{1}{3}+\frac{1}{3}$?

A. $\frac{7}{3}$

B. $7 \times \frac{1}{3}$

C. $2\frac{2}{3}$

D. $2\frac{1}{3}$

4.NF.4

4. What is $4 \times \frac{5}{6}$?

A. $\frac{10}{3}$

B. $\frac{9}{6}$

C. $4\frac{5}{6}$

D. $\frac{24}{5}$

4.NF.4

5. Alexey read for $\frac{7}{8}$ of an hour on Monday, Tuesday, Thursday and Saturday. Which expression can we use to find out how many hours Alexey read last week?

A. $\frac{7}{8} \times 4$

B. $\frac{7}{8} \times 5$

C. $\frac{7}{8} \times 3$

D. $7 \times 8 \times 4$

4.NF.4

TIP of the DAY

Tomorrow when you take the assessment, remember to read the questions carefully and think about what is being asked. If it is addition or subtraction, you'll need to find a common denominator before adding or subtracting.

WEEK 9 : DAY 5

1. Each cupcake needs $\frac{5}{8}$ of a tablespoon of frosting. How much frosting will be needed for 40 cupcakes?

   A. $40\frac{5}{8}$ tablespoons

   B. $\frac{45}{8}$ tablespoons

   C. 25 tablespoons

   D. $8\frac{5}{40}$ tablespoons

   4.NF.4

2. What is another way to write $\frac{2}{5} + \frac{2}{5} + \frac{2}{5}$?

   A. $\frac{2}{5} \times 3$

   C. $2\frac{5}{3}$

   B. $\frac{5}{2} \times 3$

   D. $3\frac{2}{5}$

   4.NF.4

3. Which expression is represented by the model below?

   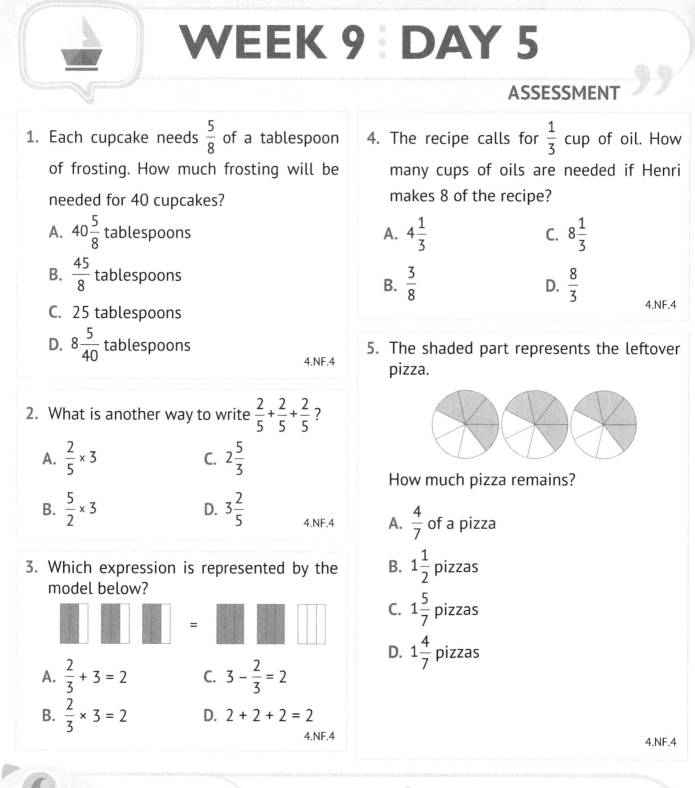

   A. $\frac{2}{3} + 3 = 2$

   C. $3 - \frac{2}{3} = 2$

   B. $\frac{2}{3} \times 3 = 2$

   D. $2 + 2 + 2 = 2$

   4.NF.4

4. The recipe calls for $\frac{1}{3}$ cup of oil. How many cups of oils are needed if Henri makes 8 of the recipe?

   A. $4\frac{1}{3}$

   C. $8\frac{1}{3}$

   B. $\frac{3}{8}$

   D. $\frac{8}{3}$

   4.NF.4

5. The shaded part represents the leftover pizza.

   How much pizza remains?

   A. $\frac{4}{7}$ of a pizza

   B. $1\frac{1}{2}$ pizzas

   C. $1\frac{5}{7}$ pizzas

   D. $1\frac{4}{7}$ pizzas

   4.NF.4

DAY 6
Challenge question

Avery rode her bike for $\frac{3}{4}$ of an hour each day during the week and then ran for $\frac{4}{5}$ of an hour on Saturday and Sunday. How many hours of exercise did Avery get last week?

4.NF.4

WEEK 10

ARGOPREP.COM

VIDEO EXPLANATIONS

The fractions in Week 10 focus on those fractions that have 10 or 100 in the denominator. These fractions can be added together and rewritten as decimals.

You can find detailed video explanations of each problem in the book by visiting:
ArgoPrep.com

1. What fraction is equivalent to $\frac{7}{10}$?

   A. $\frac{7}{1000}$ C. $\frac{70}{1000}$

   B. $\frac{7}{100}$ D. $\frac{70}{100}$

   4.NF.5

2. Add: $\frac{4}{10} + \frac{3}{100}$

   A. $\frac{43}{10}$ C. $\frac{34}{10}$

   B. $\frac{43}{100}$ D. $\frac{340}{10}$

   4.NF.5

3. What is the sum of $\frac{50}{100}$ and $\frac{5}{10}$?

   A. $\frac{55}{10}$ C. $\frac{100}{10}$

   B. $\frac{55}{100}$ D. $\frac{100}{100}$

   4.NF.5

4. What is another way to write $\frac{80}{100}$?

   A. $\frac{8}{10}$ C. $\frac{80}{10}$

   B. $\frac{8}{100}$ D. $\frac{70}{1000}$

   4.NF.5

5. Round 8,647,954 to the nearest hundred thousand.

   A. 9,000,000
   B. 8,600,000
   C. 8,650,000
   D. 8,648,000

   4.NBT.3

6. Add: $\frac{7}{10} + \frac{7}{100}$

   A. $\frac{14}{10}$ C. $\frac{77}{10}$

   B. $\frac{14}{100}$ D. $\frac{77}{100}$

   4.NF.5

TIP of the DAY

Before adding, make sure the denominators are the same. If not, change the denominators so that they are like denominators.

1. Find the sum of $\frac{1}{10}$ and $\frac{6}{100}$.

   A. $\frac{16}{10}$

   B. $\frac{16}{100}$

   C. $\frac{7}{10}$

   D. $\frac{7}{100}$

   4.NF.5

2. What fraction is equivalent to $\frac{9}{10}$?

   A. $\frac{90}{100}$

   B. $\frac{9}{100}$

   C. $\frac{1}{9}$

   D. $\frac{10}{9}$

   4.NF.5

3. What is $\frac{16}{100} + \frac{14}{100}$?

   A. $\frac{3}{10}$

   B. $\frac{3}{100}$

   C. $\frac{30}{10}$

   D. $\frac{30}{1000}$

   4.NF.5

4. What fraction is equivalent to $\frac{10}{100}$?

   A. $\frac{100}{10}$

   B. $\frac{10}{10}$

   C. $\frac{1}{100}$

   D. $\frac{1}{10}$

   4.NF.5

5. Add: $\frac{9}{10} + \frac{8}{100}$

   A. $\frac{17}{10}$

   B. $\frac{17}{100}$

   C. $\frac{98}{100}$

   D. $\frac{98}{10}$

   4.NF.5

6. Sharon baked bread and placed it in boxes that could contain 9 loaves each. If she baked 1019 loaves and could only ship full boxes, how many loaves would not be shipped?

   A. 1
   B. 2
   C. 5
   D. 6

   4.NBT.6

TIP of the DAY

By now you should be starting to see the connection between fractions that have denominators of 10 and 100.

WEEK 10 : DAY 3

1. How can $\frac{4}{100}$ be written as a decimal?

   A. 4.0
   B. 0.4
   C. 0.04
   D. 0.004

2. The snake was $\frac{37}{100}$ of a yard long. What is this length as a decimal?

   A. 3.7 yards
   B. 0.37 yards
   C. 0.037 yards
   D. 37 yards

3. Look at the number line.

   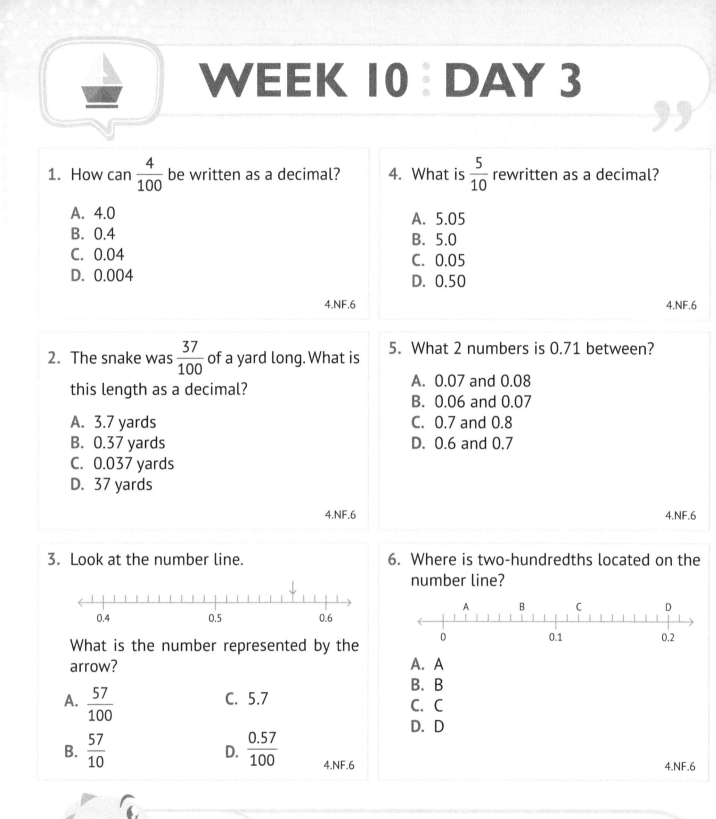

   0.4   0.5   0.6

   What is the number represented by the arrow?

   A. $\frac{57}{100}$ C. 5.7

   B. $\frac{57}{10}$ D. $\frac{0.57}{100}$

4. What is $\frac{5}{10}$ rewritten as a decimal?

   A. 5.05
   B. 5.0
   C. 0.05
   D. 0.50

5. What 2 numbers is 0.71 between?

   A. 0.07 and 0.08
   B. 0.06 and 0.07
   C. 0.7 and 0.8
   D. 0.6 and 0.7

6. Where is two-hundredths located on the number line?

   A   B   C   D

   0   0.1   0.2

   A. A
   B. B
   C. C
   D. D

TIP of the DAY

When writing decimal numbers, be sure not to confuse the tens place with the tenTHs place. Six tens = 60 but six tenths = 0.6.

1. Rewrite nine-tenths as a decimal.

   A. 0.9
   B. 0.09
   C. 0.009
   D. 9

   4.NF.6

4. What is another way to write 0.73?

   A. $\dfrac{73}{1}$

   B. $\dfrac{73}{10}$

   C. $\dfrac{73}{100}$

   D. $\dfrac{73}{1000}$

   4.NF.6

2. What is the number represented by the arrow?

   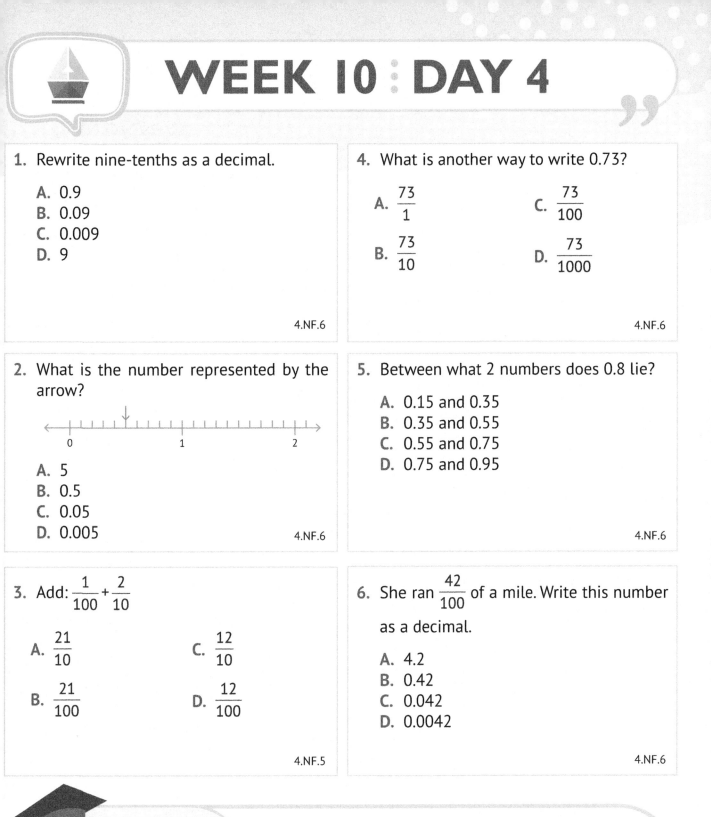

   A. 5
   B. 0.5
   C. 0.05
   D. 0.005

   4.NF.6

5. Between what 2 numbers does 0.8 lie?

   A. 0.15 and 0.35
   B. 0.35 and 0.55
   C. 0.55 and 0.75
   D. 0.75 and 0.95

   4.NF.6

3. Add: $\dfrac{1}{100} + \dfrac{2}{10}$

   A. $\dfrac{21}{10}$

   B. $\dfrac{21}{100}$

   C. $\dfrac{12}{10}$

   D. $\dfrac{12}{100}$

   4.NF.5

6. She ran $\dfrac{42}{100}$ of a mile. Write this number as a decimal.

   A. 4.2
   B. 0.42
   C. 0.042
   D. 0.0042

   4.NF.6

TIP of the DAY

You may want to review the place values so you don't forget them.

1. What is $\dfrac{5}{10} + \dfrac{4}{10}$?

   A. $\dfrac{9}{100}$

   B. $\dfrac{54}{10}$

   C. $\dfrac{54}{100}$

   D. $\dfrac{9}{10}$

   4.NF.5

2. Which fraction is equivalent to 0.2?

   A. $\dfrac{2}{1}$

   B. $\dfrac{2}{10}$

   C. $\dfrac{2}{100}$

   D. $\dfrac{2}{1000}$

   4.NF.6

3. Find the fraction that is equivalent to 0.07.

   A. $\dfrac{7}{1}$

   B. $\dfrac{7}{10}$

   C. $\dfrac{7}{100}$

   D. $\dfrac{70}{100}$

   4.NF.6

4. Find the sum of $\dfrac{4}{100}$ and $\dfrac{3}{10}$.

   A. $\dfrac{43}{10}$

   B. $\dfrac{43}{100}$

   C. $\dfrac{34}{10}$

   D. $\dfrac{34}{100}$

   4.NF.5

5. If $108 = 9 \times 12$, then 108 is 12 times as great as _____.

   A. 8

   B. 9

   C. 10

   D. 12

   4.OA.1

6. Add: $\dfrac{2}{100} + \dfrac{1}{10}$

   A. $\dfrac{12}{100}$

   B. $\dfrac{12}{10}$

   C. $\dfrac{21}{100}$

   D. $\dfrac{21}{10}$

   4.NF.5

DAY 6
Challenge question

Dimes are worth 10 pennies, and one dime can be written as $\dfrac{1}{10}$. What is the value of 3 dimes and 6 pennies?

4.NF.5
4.NF.6

70

VIDEO EXPLANATIONS ▶

ARGOPREP.COM

Last week you learned about writing decimal numbers. This week you will have an opportunity to compare these numbers using the comparison symbols <, >, and =.

You can find detailed video explanations of each problem in the book by visiting:
ArgoPrep.com

1. Chicken is $3.75 per pound and beef is $3.90 per pound. Which statement is true?

   A. 3.75 < 3.9
   B. 3.75 > 3.9
   C. 3.9 = 3.75
   D. 3.9 < 3.75

   4.NF.7

2. Below is a chart showing the time it took some students to run a mile. Which statement is true?

Student	Time (minutes)
Larry	9.16
Barry	9.3
Shari	9.7

   A. 9.7 < 9.3
   B. 9.3 > 9.7
   C. 9.16 > 9.7
   D. 9.16 < 9.3

   4.NF.7

3. Which of the numbers has the greatest value?

   A. 14.3
   B. 14.71
   C. 14.9
   D. 14.31

   4.NF.7

4. What is the product of 8 and 251?

   A. $31\frac{3}{8}$
   B. 208
   C. 259
   D. 2008

   4.NBT.5

5. Is the statement below correct? Why or why not?

   $$8.7 = 8.70$$

   A. It is correct because there is an 8 before the decimal.

   B. The statement is correct because $8\frac{7}{10}$ is equal to $8\frac{70}{100}$.

   C. It is incorrect because there are a different number of digits in the 2 numbers.

   D. It is incorrect because 7 does not equal 70.

   4.NF.7

TIP of the DAY

Recall that $\frac{3}{10}$ is equal to $\frac{30}{100}$ so 0.3 is equal to 0.30.

1. Which of the following statements is true?

   A. 12.4 < 12.40
   B. 18.73 > 18.8
   C. 24.1 = 24.10
   D. 32 < 31.9

   4.NF.7

2. Mary needs to spend less than $3.80 on milk. Which milk can she **NOT** buy?

Kind of milk	Price (dollars)
Chocolate	3.76
Almond	3.9
Whole	3.59
Skim	3.48

   A. Chocolate
   B. Almond
   C. Whole
   D. Skim

   4.NF.7

3. Which of these numbers is the smallest?

   A. 17.09
   B. 17.1
   C. 17.26
   D. 17.03

   4.NF.7

4. Which number sentence does the model represent?

   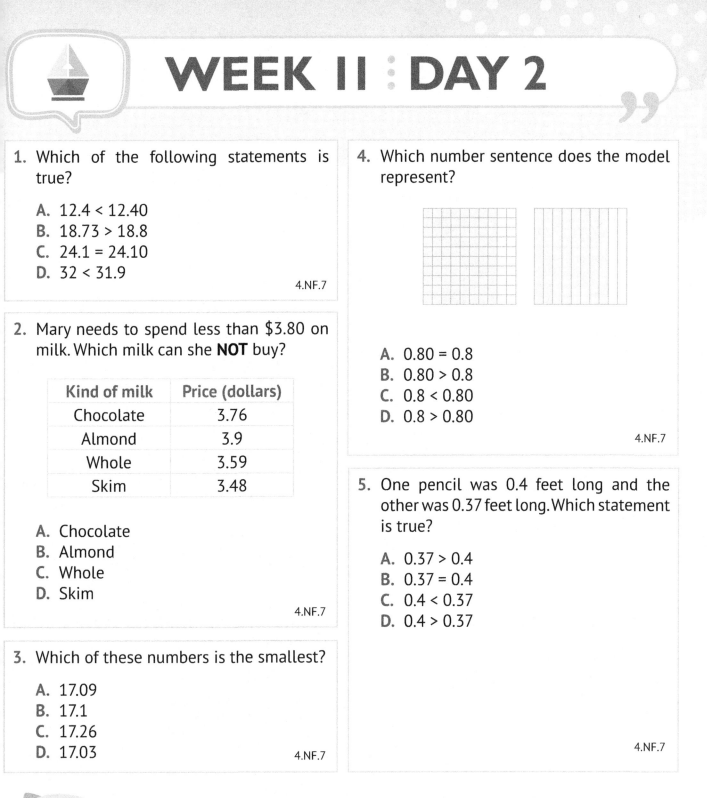

   A. 0.80 = 0.8
   B. 0.80 > 0.8
   C. 0.8 < 0.80
   D. 0.8 > 0.80

   4.NF.7

5. One pencil was 0.4 feet long and the other was 0.37 feet long. Which statement is true?

   A. 0.37 > 0.4
   B. 0.37 = 0.4
   C. 0.4 < 0.37
   D. 0.4 > 0.37

   4.NF.7

TIP of the DAY

Decimal numbers are used everyday when people use money. Next time your family buys something, see if you can change the dollar amount into a decimal number.

1. Look at the model below.

What number sentence does the model represent?

A. 0.47 < 0.5
B. 0.47 > 0.5
C. 0.5 = 0.47
D. 0.5 < 0.47

4.NF.7

2. Which number has the greatest value?

A. 13.54
B. 13.6
C. 13.09
D. 13.4

4.NF.7

3. Which number sentence is represented by the model below?

A. 0.3 = 0.32
B. 0.3 > 0.32
C. 0.32 < 0.3
D. 0.32 > 0.3

4.NF.7

4. The worm traveled 0.46 inches and the ant traveled 0.5 inches. Which statement is true?

A. 0.5 < 0.46   C. 0.46 < 0.5
B. 0.5 = 0.46   D. 0.46 > 0.5

4.NF.7

5. Which set of numbers contains ONLY prime numbers?

A. 3, 13, 23, 33, 43
B. 2, 5, 11, 17, 32
C. 1, 3, 7, 19, 29
D. 2, 11, 19, 29, 37

4.OA.4

TIP of the DAY

When comparing numbers, don't forget the place values. An 8 in the tenths place has a greater value than an 8 in the hundredths place so 0.8 > 0.08.

1. James has 70 cents and Renee has 69 cents. Which number sentence is true?

   A. 0.7 < 0.69
   B. 0.7 = 0.69
   C. 0.69 < 0.7
   D. 0.69 > 0.7

   4.NF.7

2. Missy was training for the 100 meter race. Her times (in seconds) are below.

Trial	Time
1	11.3
2	11.26
3	11.33
4	11.29

   Which trial was her fastest time?

   A. 1
   B. 2
   C. 3
   D. 4

   4.NF.7

3. Using the models below, which number sentence is true?

   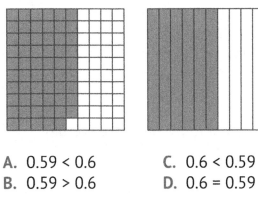

   A. 0.59 < 0.6   C. 0.6 < 0.59
   B. 0.59 > 0.6   D. 0.6 = 0.59

   4.NF.7

4. The Jasmine bush had 12 times as many blooms as the Rose bush, which had 8 blooms. Let j equal the number of blooms on the Jasmine bush. Which equation can be used to find the number of Jasmine blooms?

   A. $j = 8 \div 12$
   B. $j = 8 - 12$
   C. $j = 8 + 12$
   D. $j = 8 \times 12$

   4.OA.2

5. Which number is the smallest?

   A. 34.2   C. 34.1
   B. 34.07   D. 34.17

   4.NF.7

TIP of the DAY

Recall that 0.13 < 0.2 because 0.2 actually means twenty hundredths, which is larger than thirteen hundredths.

1. Which number is the largest?

   A. 91
   B. 90.08
   C. 90.77
   D. 90.9

   4.NF.7

2. Which number sentence is true?

   A. 36.08 > 36.1
   B. 27 < 26.99
   C. 47.2 = 47.22
   D. 65.8 = 65.80

   4.NF.7

3. Use the given models to find the true statement.

   A. 0.36 > 0.4
   B. 0.36 < 0.4
   C. 0.4 = 0.36
   D. 0.4 < 0.36

   4.NF.7

4. Find the number that has the smallest value.

   A. 3.04
   B. 3.4
   C. 3.41
   D. 4.01

   4.NF.7

5. Which number is a multiple of both 9 and 6?

   A. 27
   B. 36
   C. 42
   D. 45

   4.OA.4

6. Which number has the largest value?

   A. 112.09
   B. 112.1
   C. 112.2
   D. 112.17

   4.NF.7

DAY 6
Challenge question

Dimes are worth 10 pennies, or $0.10. Write a true comparison statement using 7 dimes and 46 pennies.

4.NF.7

WEEK 12

ARGOPREP.COM

: VIDEO
EXPLANATIONS ▶

Inches, feet, yards and miles – all of these measurement units and many others will be used in Week 12 exercises. This week you'll work on changing from one unit of measure to another. But be careful – make sure you know whether you are using metric units or other units!

You can find detailed video explanations of each problem in the book by visiting: ArgoPrep.com

1. How many times longer is 1 foot than 1 inch?

   A. 2
   B. 6
   C. 12
   D. 18

   4.MD.1

4. Hannah took 5 minutes to run the laps in gym. How many seconds are in 5 minutes?

   A. 3000 seconds
   B. 300 seconds
   C. 60 seconds
   D. 30 seconds

   4.MD.1

2. How many ounces are in 4 pounds?

   A. 16
   B. 32
   C. 48
   D. 64

   4.MD.1

5. How many millimeters are in 3 meters?

   A. 3000
   B. 300
   C. 30
   D. $\dfrac{1}{300}$

   4.MD.1

3. How many times larger is a kilometer than a meter?

   A. 10 times
   B. 100 times
   C. 1000 times
   D. 1 time

   4.MD.1

6. If Sheila ran 5,280 feet, how many miles did she run?

   A. $\dfrac{1}{2}$
   B. 1
   C. 2
   D. 10

   4.MD.1

TIP of the DAY

Be sure to use the right unit conversions when working with measurements such as miles, meters or minutes.

1. Which statement is true?

   A. 20 cm = 2 km
   B. 2 km = 200 cm
   C. 2000 m = 2 km
   D. 200 mm = 2 cm

   4.MD.1

2. How many hours are in 1 week?

   A. 24
   B. 72
   C. 120
   D. 168

   4.MD.1

3. Patrick needs 14 yards of material. How many feet of material will he need?

   A. $4\frac{2}{3}$
   B. 17
   C. 28
   D. 42

   4.MD.1

4. Look at the table below.

Yards	Miles
3520	2
5280	3

   Which ordered pair would complete the table above?

   A. (1760, 1)
   B. (1, 1760)
   C. (1, 1000)
   D. (1000, 1)

   4.MD.1

5. What is $\dfrac{4}{100} + \dfrac{7}{10}$?

   A. $\dfrac{47}{10}$ C. $\dfrac{74}{10}$

   B. $\dfrac{47}{100}$ D. $\dfrac{74}{100}$

   4.NF.5

TIP of the DAY

Remember that the Metric System uses 10 as its factor. The U.S. System of Weights and Measures does not have a consistent factor so pay extra attention when working on units other than metric units.

1. How many times longer is a mile than a yard?

   A. 100
   B. 1000
   C. 1,760
   D. 5,280

   4.MD.1

2. How many minutes are in 3 hours?

   A. 30
   B. 60
   C. 120
   D. 180

   4.MD.1

3. Jerome caught a fish that was 1 meter long. How many centimeters long was it?

   A. 1,000
   B. 10,000
   C. 10
   D. 100

   4.MD.1

4. Look at the table below.

Kilometers	Meters
1	1,000
3	
4	4,000

   Which number would complete the table above?

   A. 2,000
   B. 3,000
   C. 200
   D. 300

   4.MD.1

5. The hose was a yard long. How many inches long was the hose?

   A. 12
   B. 24
   C. 36
   D. 100

   4.MD.1

6. How many seconds are in one day?

   A. 60
   B. 1,440
   C. 3,600
   D. 86,400

   4.MD.1

TIP *of the* **DAY**

Memorize the basic unit conversions.
1 meter = 100 centimeters = 1,000 millimeters

1. How many times greater is one mile than one foot?

   A. 100
   B. 1000
   C. 1,760
   D. 5,280

   4.MD.1

2. Gwyneth had 2.5 minutes to complete her laps. How many seconds did she have?

   A. 63
   B. 120
   C. 150
   D. 180

   4.MD.1

3. Conner's car traveled 40 kilometers. How many meters did it travel?

   A. 40,000
   B. 4,000
   C. 400
   D. 40

   4.MD.1

4. Look at the table below.

Inches	Yards
36	1
108	3

   Which ordered pair would complete the table above?

   A. 72, 2
   B. 80, 2
   C. 88, 2
   D. 96, 2

   4.MD.1

5. The mass of the bell was 3 kilograms. How many grams was the bell?

   A. 3,000
   B. 300
   C. 30
   D. 3

   4.MD.1

TIP of the DAY

If you are changing to smaller units, you will need more of them to measure the same thing.

1. Adrian had 4 days to complete the assignment. How many hours did she have?

    A. 72
    B. 96
    C. 120
    D. 148

    4.MD.1

2. There was a rug that measured 9 feet long. How many inches long was the rug?

    A. 21
    B. 27
    C. 108
    D. 120

    4.MD.1

3. How many centiliters are in 2 liters?

    A. 20
    B. 200
    C. 2,000
    D. 20,000

    4.MD.1

4. Which expression is NOT a way to write $\frac{8}{5}$?

    A. $\frac{8}{5} + \frac{8}{5} + \frac{8}{5} + \frac{8}{5} + \frac{8}{5}$

    B. $8 \times \frac{1}{5}$

    C. $\frac{1}{5} + \frac{1}{5} + \frac{1}{5} + \frac{1}{5} + \frac{1}{5} + \frac{1}{5} + \frac{1}{5} + \frac{1}{5}$

    D. $\frac{1}{5} \times 8$

    4.NF.3

5. Look at the table below.

Pounds	Ounces
1	16
2	
4	64

    Which number would complete the table above?

    A. 22
    B. 32
    C. 44
    D. 56

    4.MD.1

DAY 6
Challenge question

Mrs. Douglas bought $3\frac{1}{4}$ pounds of bacon. How many ounces of bacon did she purchase?

4.MD.1

WEEK 13

ARGOPREP.COM

: VIDEO
EXPLANATIONS ▶

It gets real in Week 13. You will use all kinds of operations (adding, subtracting, multiplying and/or dividing) to solve word problems that use measurements such as units for time, money, length, area, and perimeter in the real world.

You can find detailed video explanations of each problem in the book by visiting:
ArgoPrep.com

1. Jill ran to the park 2.5 miles away. Dan also ran to the park and he said he ran 4,400 yards. Who ran farther and how do you know?

   A. Jill ran farther because miles are longer than yards.
   B. Dan ran farther because he ran 4,400 units and Jill only ran 2.5 units.
   C. Jill ran farther because she ran miles and Dan only ran yards.
   D. They ran the same distance because 2.5 miles is 4,400 yards.

   4.MD.2

2. There was a cooler that held 10 liters. Each cup can hold $\frac{1}{2}$ liter. How many cups can be filled from the cooler?

   A. 5
   B. 10
   C. 20
   D. 100

   4.MD.2

3. There were some vitamins that were 1 mg per pill. The bottle held 1 gram of medicine. How many vitamins were in the bottle?

   A. 10
   B. 100
   C. 1,000
   D. 10,000

   4.MD.2

4. Jordan is 63 inches tall and Sam is 5.5 feet tall. Who is taller and how do you know?

   A. Sam is taller because 66 in > 63 in.
   B. Sam is taller because feet are longer than inches.
   C. Jordan is taller because 63 > 5.5.
   D. Jordan is taller because 63 inches is longer than 5.5 feet.

   4.MD.2

5. Katie and Thomas each had a piece of string that they measured. The measurements are shown below.

   | Katie | 18 inches |
   | Thomas | 1.5 yards |

   Who had the longer string? State your reasoning.

   A. Thomas' string was longer because yards is longer than inches.
   B. Thomas' string was longer because 1.5 yards is 54 inches.
   C. Katie's string was longer because she had 18 units and Thomas only had 1.5.
   D. Their strings are the same length because 18 inches equals 1.5 yards.

   4.MD.2

6. Leah needed 5 meters of leather for her project but she only had a ruler with centimeters on it. How many centimeters of leather did Leah need?

   4.MD.2

   A. 0.05   B. 0.5   C. 50   D. 500

1. Circuit Rider was on the Appalachian Trail for 4 days. Princess was on the trail for 92 hours. Who was hiking the longest? Prove your answer.

   A. Princess hiked the longest because 92 > 4.
   B. Circuit Rider hiked longer because 4 days = 96 hours and 96 > 92.
   C. They hiked the same amount of time because 4 days = 92 hours.
   D. Princess hiked longer because 92 hours is 5 days.

   4.MD.2

2. Using the rule "subtract 2", which number is next in the pattern?

   39, 37, 35, _____

   A. 37   C. 33
   B. 34   D. 32

   4.OA.5

3. Joel ran 8 kilometers in the race. Kendra wanted to know how many meters were in 8 kilometers. What would you tell Kendra?

   A. 0.08   C. 800
   B. 80   D. 8000

   4.MD.2

4. One cup had a mass of 5 grams. What is the mass of 21 cups?

   A. 105 mg
   B. 1,050 mg
   C. 10,500 mg
   D. 105,000 mg

   4.MD.2

5. Janet is auditioning for a play in 6 days. How many hours does she have to prepare?

   A. 24
   B. 72
   C. 144
   D. 168

   4.MD.2

6. Frank lost 2 pounds. Joan lost 33 ounces. Who lost the most weight? Prove your answer.

   A. Frank lost more because he lost pounds and pounds > ounces.
   B. They lost the same amount because 2 pounds = 33 ounces.
   C. Joan lost more because 33 > 2.
   D. Joan lost more because 2 pounds is 32 ounces and she lost 33.

   4.MD.2

TIP of the DAY

In word problems, be sure to answer the question being asked.

1. Find the length of a room that is 10 feet wide and has a perimeter of 34 feet.

   A. 7 feet
   B. 14 feet
   C. 24 feet
   D. 44 feet

   4.MD.3

2. The area of the hallway shown below is 72 square meters. How long is the length?

   4 meters

   length?

   A. 12 meters
   B. 18 meters
   C. 32 meters
   D. 64 meters

   4.MD.3

3. A square piece of carpet has an area of 36 square inches. What is its perimeter?

   A. 6 inches
   B. 9 inches
   C. 18 inches
   D. 24 inches

   4.MD.3

4. Clare measured a rectangular room but lost some of the measurements. Here is the information that he can find:

Length	Width	Perimeter	Area
	9		225

   Complete the table above.

   All measurements are in feet

   A. Length = 25; Perimeter = 34
   B. Length = 50; Perimeter = 116
   C. Length = 25; Perimeter = 68
   D. Length = 50; Perimeter = 68

   4.MD.3

5. The branch is a yard long. How many inches long is the branch?

   A. 12
   B. 24
   C. 36
   D. 100

   4.MD.1

6. A rectangular deck has a perimeter of 40 meters with a width of 8 meters. What is the area of the deck (in square meters)?

   A. 8   C. 96
   B. 12   D. 320

   4.MD.3

TIP
of the
DAY

Remember that area uses square units such as square inches, square centimeters and squares miles. Length (which includes perimeter) is measured in linear units such as inches, centimeters and miles.

1. A rectangular stage had a perimeter of 150 yards. The length was 50 yards. What was the width of the stage?

   A. 25 yards
   B. 50 yards
   C. 75 yards
   D. 100 yards

   4.MD.3

2. The area of a baby blanket is 864 in². The length is 36 inches, what is the width?

   A. 12 inches
   B. 24 inches
   C. 216 inches
   D. 396 inches

   4.MD.3

3. The rectangular pool has a length of 27 feet and a perimeter of 94 feet. What is its area (in square feet)?

   A. 20
   B. 135
   C. 270
   D. 540

   4.MD.3

4. Alyssa was sewing a placemat and needed to know how much binding to put around the edges. If the width was 20 cm and the area was 700 cm², how much binding was needed (in cm)?

   A. 35
   B. 55
   C. 110
   D. 220

   4.MD.3

5. A rectangular billboard had an area of 450 square meters. If the height was 18, what was the length (in meters)?

   A. 12.5
   B. 25
   C. 189
   D. 207

   4.MD.3

6. Which statement is true?

   A. $7 \times 10{,}000 + 6 \times 100 > 8 \times 10{,}000$
   B. 5 hundreds + 3 tens < 4 hundreds + 11 tens
   C. $3.19 < 3.2$
   D. $26 \times 71 > 4{,}368 - 1{,}902$

   4.NBT.2

TIP of the DAY

Approach word problems one step at a time.

WEEK 13 : DAY 5

ASSESSMENT

1. Patti had 60 liters of tea. How many mL of tea did Patti have?

   A. 6
   B. 600
   C. 6,000
   D. 60,000

   4.MD.2

2. The dining room has a perimeter of 76 feet and a width of 16 feet. How much carpet would be needed to carpet the entire room?

   A. 352 square feet
   B. 528 square feet
   C. 608 square feet
   D. 1,216 square feet

   4.MD.3

3. The rug had an edge that totaled 140 inches. Its length was 54 inches. What was its area?

   A. 432 in^2
   B. 864 in^2
   C. 1,728 in^2
   D. 7,560 in^2

   4.MD.3

4. A rectangular deck has a perimeter of 24 yards and length of 8 yards. What is the area of the deck?

   A. 32 ft^2
   B. 72 ft^2
   C. 180 ft^2
   D. 288 ft^2

   4.MD.3

5. The weight of 3 dogs is shown below.

Dog	Pounds
1	19
2	35
3	24

   If all 3 dogs were placed on a scale, how much would the scale read, in ounces?

   A. 94
   B. 234
   C. 780
   D. 1,248

   4.MD.2

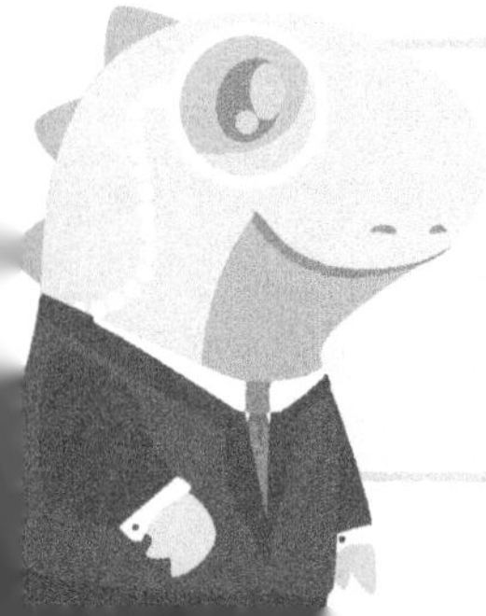

DAY 6
Challenge question

The athletic field had an area of 5000 yds^2. One length of the field was 50 yards. What was the perimeter of the field?

4.MD.3

WEEK 14

VIDEO EXPLANATIONS ► ARGOPREP.COM

Like to draw or look at pictures? If so, you'll love Week 14! Here you will see and use information that is given in tables or shown on charts. Be sure to read all of the titles and information given to help you understand what the numbers mean.

You can find detailed video explanations of each problem in the book by visiting: ArgoPrep.com

Ms. Brown's 4th graders brought in boxes and then measured them in feet. The results are below. Use the following data set to answer questions 1–3.

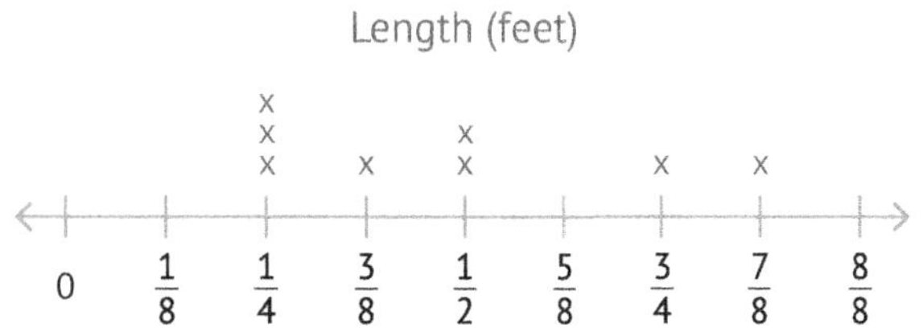

Length (feet)

1. Looking at the data above, how many students participated in the activity?

   A. 6   B. 8   C. 10   D. 12

   4.MD.4

2. What is the difference in length between the longest box and the shortest box?

   A. $\frac{7}{8}$ B. $\frac{6}{8}$ C. $\frac{5}{8}$ D. $\frac{3}{4}$

   4.MD.4

3. What is the measurement of the greatest amount of boxes?

   A. $\frac{1}{4}$ B. $\frac{3}{8}$ C. $\frac{1}{2}$ D. $\frac{3}{4}$

   4.MD.4

The soccer team was asked to bring sports drinks to the tournament. The amounts (in gallons) that each team member brought are shown below. Use the following data set to answer questions 4–6.

Sports drink (gallons)

4. How much sports drink was collected altogether?

   A. 11 gallons   C. $17\frac{1}{2}$ gallons

   B. $15\frac{1}{2}$ gallons   D. 20 gallons

   4.MD.4

5. If every player was counted in the data, how many players were on the team?

   A. 9   B. 10   C. 11   D. 12

   4.MD.4

6. What was the largest amount that any player brought (in gallons)?

   A. $1\frac{1}{2}$ B. 2   C. $2\frac{1}{2}$ D. 3

   4.MD.4

TIP of the DAY

When looking at data sets, pay close attention to the labels and any other clues the diagrams/charts provide.

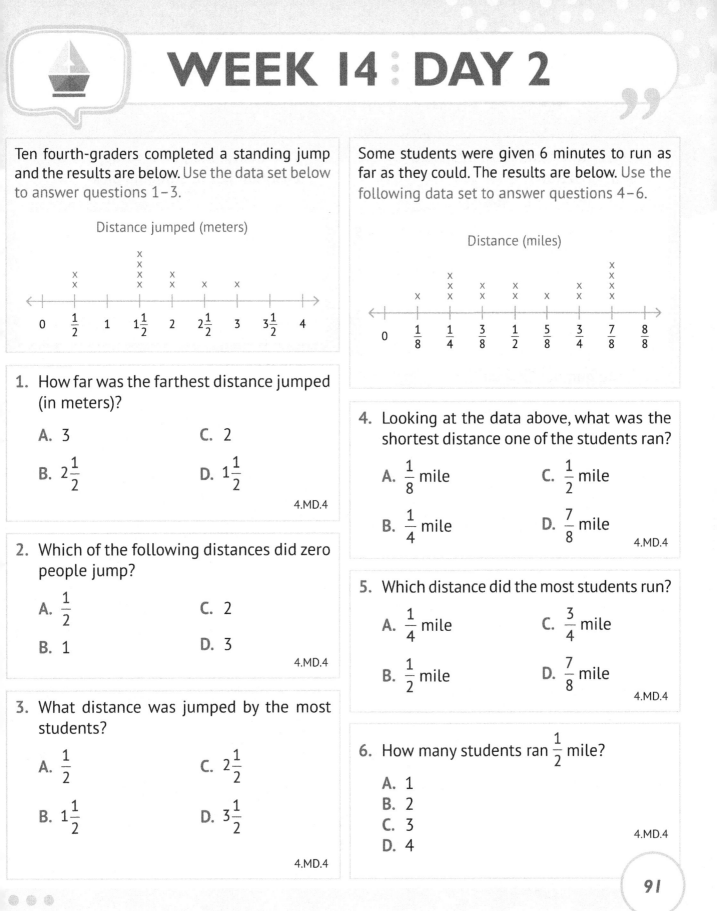

Ten fourth-graders completed a standing jump and the results are below. **Use the data set below to answer questions 1–3.**

Distance jumped (meters)

Some students were given 6 minutes to run as far as they could. The results are below. **Use the following data set to answer questions 4–6.**

Distance (miles)

1. How far was the farthest distance jumped (in meters)?

   A. 3

   C. 2

   B. $2\frac{1}{2}$

   D. $1\frac{1}{2}$

   4.MD.4

2. Which of the following distances did zero people jump?

   A. $\frac{1}{2}$

   C. 2

   B. 1

   D. 3

   4.MD.4

3. What distance was jumped by the most students?

   A. $\frac{1}{2}$

   C. $2\frac{1}{2}$

   B. $1\frac{1}{2}$

   D. $3\frac{1}{2}$

   4.MD.4

4. Looking at the data above, what was the shortest distance one of the students ran?

   A. $\frac{1}{8}$ mile

   C. $\frac{1}{2}$ mile

   B. $\frac{1}{4}$ mile

   D. $\frac{7}{8}$ mile

   4.MD.4

5. Which distance did the most students run?

   A. $\frac{1}{4}$ mile

   C. $\frac{3}{4}$ mile

   B. $\frac{1}{2}$ mile

   D. $\frac{7}{8}$ mile

   4.MD.4

6. How many students ran $\frac{1}{2}$ mile?

   A. 1
   B. 2
   C. 3
   D. 4

   4.MD.4

1. Which statement is represented by the equation below?

$$14 \times 4 = 56$$

A. The number 14 is 4 times as many as the number 56.

B. The number 14 is 4 more than the number 56.

C. The number 56 is 4 more than the number 14.

D. The number 56 is 4 times as many as the number 14.

4.OA.1

Mrs. Hamrick's class went on a field trip to pick apples. The data set below shows how many kilograms of apples each student picked. Use it to answer questions 2–4.

Apples picked (Kg)

2. How many students went apple picking?

A. 21   C. 25

B. 23   D. 27

4.MD.4

---

3. How many kilograms of apples did the least number of students pick?

A. 1

B. 2

C. 3

D. 4

4.MD.4

---

4. How many more students picked 2 kilograms of apples than picked 1 kilogram?

A. 2   C. 4

B. 3   D. 5

4.MD.4

---

5. Use the table below to answer the question that follows.

Millimeters	Centimeters
1000	100
3000	300

Which ordered pair would complete the table above?

A. (200, 2000)

B. (2000, 200)

C. (200, 20)

D. (20, 200)

4.MD.1

TIP of the DAY

When reading dot plots, be sure to understand what each dot represents.

1. What is $\dfrac{3}{10} + \dfrac{6}{100}$?

   A. $\dfrac{36}{100}$

   B. $\dfrac{36}{110}$

   C. $\dfrac{9}{10}$

   D. $\dfrac{9}{100}$

   4.NF.5

Dory tracked the rainfall over several days. The rainfall amounts are shown below. Use the data set to answer questions 2–4.

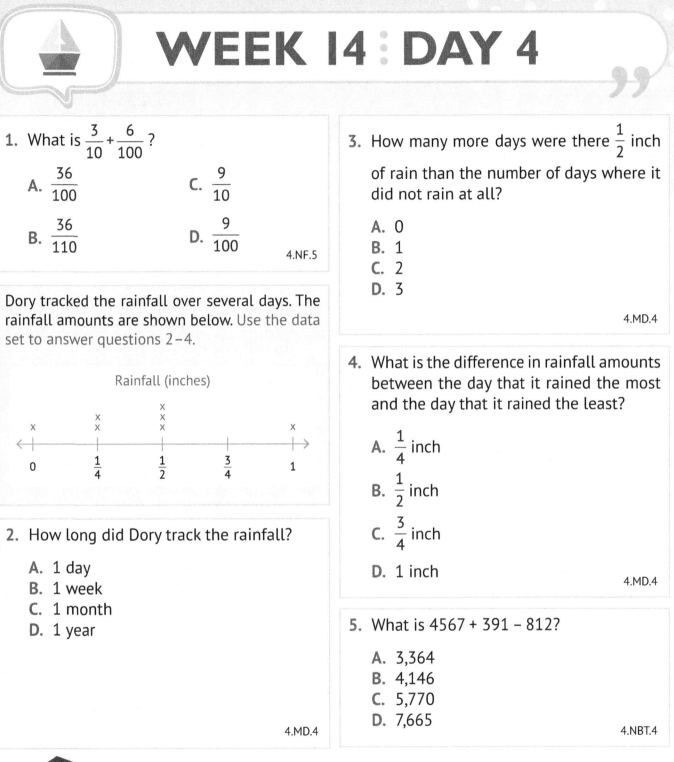

Rainfall (inches)

2. How long did Dory track the rainfall?

   A. 1 day
   B. 1 week
   C. 1 month
   D. 1 year

   4.MD.4

3. How many more days were there $\dfrac{1}{2}$ inch of rain than the number of days where it did not rain at all?

   A. 0
   B. 1
   C. 2
   D. 3

   4.MD.4

4. What is the difference in rainfall amounts between the day that it rained the most and the day that it rained the least?

   A. $\dfrac{1}{4}$ inch

   B. $\dfrac{1}{2}$ inch

   C. $\dfrac{3}{4}$ inch

   D. 1 inch

   4.MD.4

5. What is 4567 + 391 – 812?

   A. 3,364
   B. 4,146
   C. 5,770
   D. 7,665

   4.NBT.4

TIP of the DAY

Remember that graphs and charts show real information. Try to understand what the information is saying.

Twenty football players drank some water during practice. How much water they drank is shown below. Use the data set to answer questions 1–4.

Water (gallons)

| | | 0 | $\frac{1}{8}$ | $\frac{1}{4}$ | $\frac{3}{8}$ | $\frac{1}{2}$ | $\frac{5}{8}$ | $\frac{3}{4}$ | $\frac{7}{8}$ | $\frac{8}{8}$ |

1. How many players drank $\frac{1}{2}$ gallon of water?

   A. 2
   B. 3
   C. 4
   D. 5

   4.MD.4

2. How many players drank MORE than $\frac{1}{2}$ gallon?

   A. 2
   B. 3
   C. 10
   D. 15

   4.MD.4

3. How many players drank LESS than $\frac{1}{2}$ gallon?

   A. 0
   B. 2
   C. 3
   D. 5

   4.MD.4

4. What was the difference between the most water drunk and the least water drunk (in gallons)?

   A. $\frac{1}{2}$

   B. $\frac{3}{4}$

   C. $\frac{7}{8}$

   D. $\frac{8}{8}$

   4.MD.4

5. Fiona drove for 3 hours. Felipe drove for 5 hours. How many minutes did they drive altogether?

   A. 480
   B. 240
   C. 68
   D. 8

   4.MD.2

DAY 6
Challenge question

There was a watermelon-eating contest. Here are the amounts of whole watermelons that the contestants ate. Use the data to create a dot plot.

$\frac{1}{8}, \frac{1}{4}, \frac{3}{4}, \frac{1}{2}, \frac{1}{4}, \frac{1}{2}, \frac{5}{8}, \frac{5}{8}, \frac{3}{8}, \frac{1}{2}, \frac{3}{8}, \frac{3}{4}, \frac{1}{2}, \frac{3}{8}, \frac{1}{2}$

4.MD.4

WEEK 15

Angles, angles and more angles for Week 15! You'll be able to measure angles, find missing measurements, and use circles to understand what "piece" of a circle of a certain angle is.

You can find detailed video explanations of each problem in the book by visiting:
ArgoPrep.com

1. How many degrees is the angle formed by the hands on this clock?

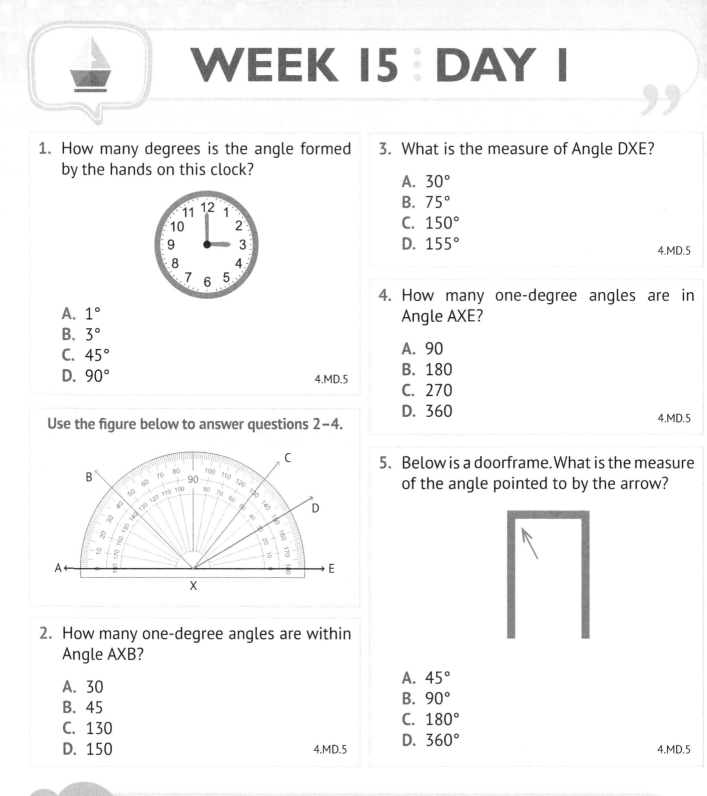

A. 1°
B. 3°
C. 45°
D. 90°

4.MD.5

Use the figure below to answer questions 2–4.

2. How many one-degree angles are within Angle AXB?

A. 30
B. 45
C. 130
D. 150

4.MD.5

3. What is the measure of Angle DXE?

A. 30°
B. 75°
C. 150°
D. 155°

4.MD.5

4. How many one-degree angles are in Angle AXE?

A. 90
B. 180
C. 270
D. 360

4.MD.5

5. Below is a doorframe. What is the measure of the angle pointed to by the arrow?

A. 45°
B. 90°
C. 180°
D. 360°

4.MD.5

TIP of the DAY

When measuring angles, be sure to use the correct row of numbers.

1. What is the measure of the angle formed by the hands on a clock when it is 6:00?

   A. 45°
   B. 90°
   C. 180°
   D. 270°

   4.MD.5

2. What is the measure of the angle formed by the shape below?

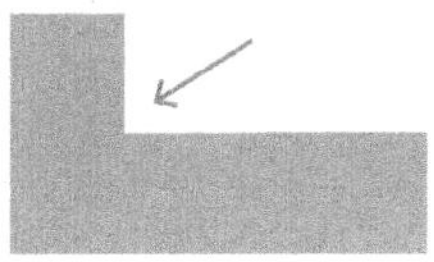

   A. 90°
   B. 180°
   C. 270°
   D. 360°

   4.MD.5

3. There is an angle that turns through 57 one-degree angles. What is the angle's measure?

   A. 57°
   B. 107°
   C. 127°
   D. 157°

   4.MD.5

Use the figure below to answer questions 4–5.

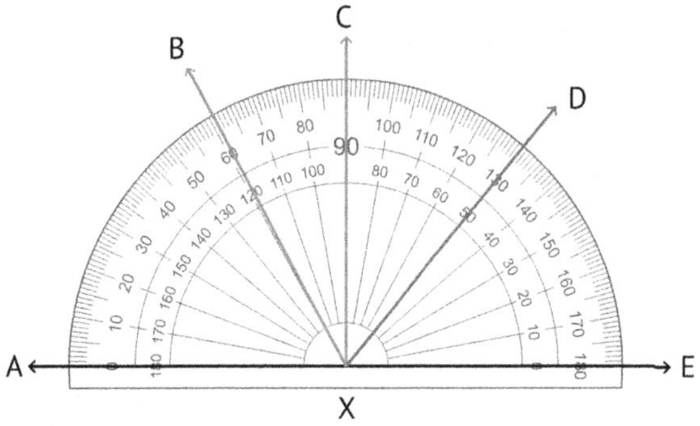

C
B
D
90
A
X
E

4. How many one-degree angles are in Angle AXD?

   A. 50
   B. 90
   C. 110
   D. 130

   4.MD.5

5. How many one-degree angles are in Angle BXA?

   A. 30
   B. 60
   C. 90
   D. 120

   4.MD.5

TIP *of the* **DAY**

Notice that the number of one-degree angles in an angle is the same number of degrees of that angle.

1. Jason was in a revolving door. He turned the door so that it would completely go around one time. How many degrees did the door turn?

   A. 90
   B. 180
   C. 270
   D. 360

   4.MD.5

Use the drawing below to answer questions 4–5.

30°

4.MD.5

2. Which set of numbers contains ALL the factors of 33?

   A. 1, 3, 11, 33
   B. 1, 33
   C. 1, 3, 7, 11, 33
   D. 1, 7, 11, 33

   4.OA.4

4. How many one-degree angles are in the 30-degree angle shown?

   A. 30
   B. 60
   C. 90
   D. 120

   4.MD.5

3. What is the measure of the angle formed by the shape below?

   A. 90°
   B. 180°
   C. 270°
   D. 360°

   4.MD.5

5. If the 30-degree angle is on the inside, how many one-degree angles are on the outside?

   A. 60
   B. 270
   C. 330
   D. 360

   4.MD.5

TIP of the DAY

Remember there are 360° in a circle.

1. Which do you NOT NEED to make an angle?

   A. 2 rays
   B. line
   C. degrees
   D. common endpoint

   4.MD.5

Use the drawing below to answer questions 2–3.

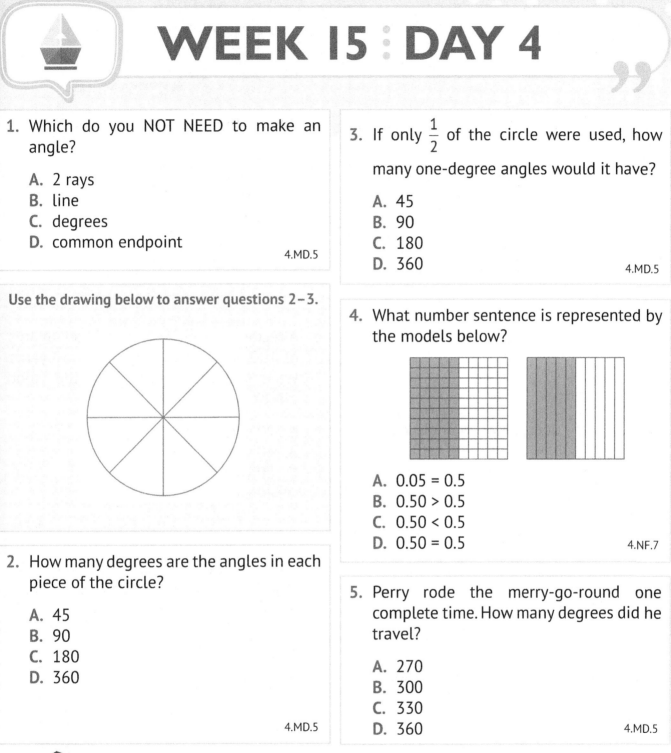

2. How many degrees are the angles in each piece of the circle?

   A. 45
   B. 90
   C. 180
   D. 360

   4.MD.5

3. If only $\frac{1}{2}$ of the circle were used, how many one-degree angles would it have?

   A. 45
   B. 90
   C. 180
   D. 360

   4.MD.5

4. What number sentence is represented by the models below?

   A. 0.05 = 0.5
   B. 0.50 > 0.5
   C. 0.50 < 0.5
   D. 0.50 = 0.5

   4.NF.7

5. Perry rode the merry-go-round one complete time. How many degrees did he travel?

   A. 270
   B. 300
   C. 330
   D. 360

   4.MD.5

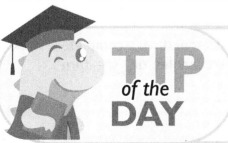

TIP of the DAY

If there are 360 degrees in a circle, there are 180 degrees in $\frac{1}{2}$ of a circle.

Use the square below to answer questions 1–3.

W

V Z X

Y

1. How many degrees are in Angle WZY?

A. 90°
B. 180°
C. 270°
D. 360°

4.MD.5

2. How many one-degree angles are in Angle VZY?

A. 90
B. 180
C. 300
D. 360

4.MD.5

3. What is the measure of Angle VYX?

A. 90°
B. 180°
C. 270°
D. 360°

4.MD.5

4. A rectangular piece of wood had an area of 100 yards². The length was 20 yards. What was the perimeter of the wood piece?

A. 20 yards
B. 40 yards
C. 50 yards
D. 80 yards

4.MD.3

5. There is an angle that turns through 121 one-degree angles. What is the angle's measure?

A. 21°
B. 71°
C. 121°
D. 181°

4.MD.5

DAY 6
Challenge question

Ivy rode the merry-go-round around in 3 complete circles. How many one-degree angles did she turn through?

4.MD.5

WEEK 16

ARGOPREP.COM

VIDEO
EXPLANATIONS ▶

Week 16 is additional practice with angles. You'll have lots of opportunities to measure angles that are given and also to think about how you would make an angle if you were given its degrees.

You can find detailed video explanations of each problem in the book by visiting:
ArgoPrep.com

Use the figure below to answer questions 1–3.

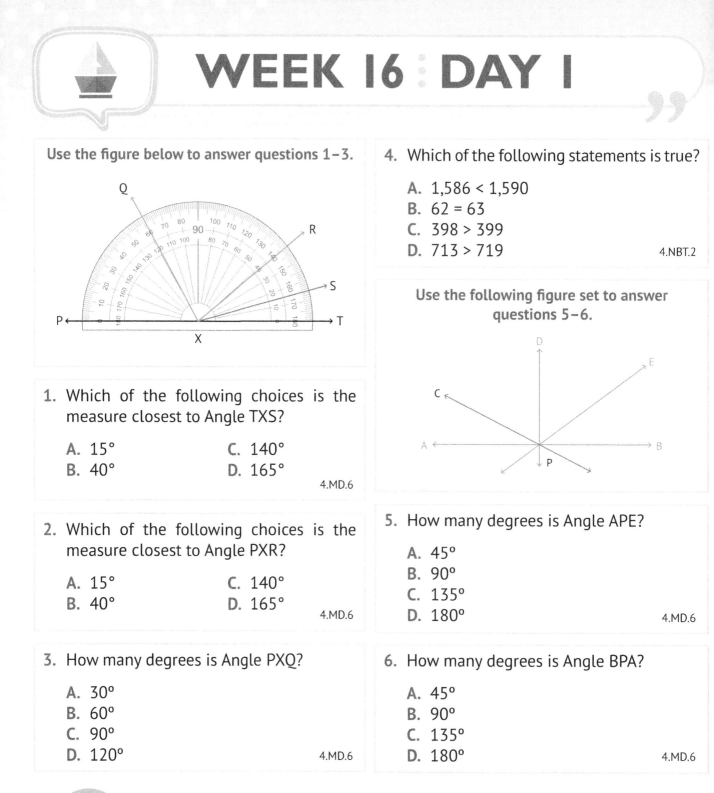

1. Which of the following choices is the measure closest to Angle TXS?

   A. 15° C. 140°
   B. 40° D. 165°

   4.MD.6

2. Which of the following choices is the measure closest to Angle PXR?

   A. 15° C. 140°
   B. 40° D. 165°

   4.MD.6

3. How many degrees is Angle PXQ?

   A. 30°
   B. 60°
   C. 90°
   D. 120°

   4.MD.6

4. Which of the following statements is true?

   A. 1,586 < 1,590
   B. 62 = 63
   C. 398 > 399
   D. 713 > 719

   4.NBT.2

Use the following figure set to answer questions 5–6.

5. How many degrees is Angle APE?

   A. 45°
   B. 90°
   C. 135°
   D. 180°

   4.MD.6

6. How many degrees is Angle BPA?

   A. 45°
   B. 90°
   C. 135°
   D. 180°

   4.MD.6

TIP of the DAY

When measuring angles, be sure to check the baseline is lined up on one of the angle's rays and that the vertex is at the part labeled "center" on the protractor.

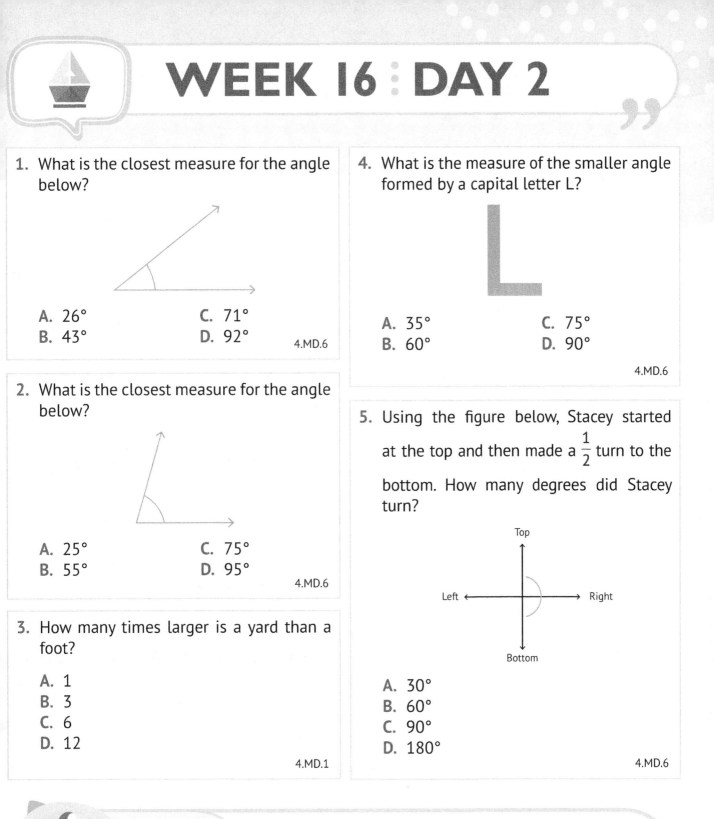

1. What is the closest measure for the angle below?

   A. 26° C. 71°
   B. 43° D. 92°

   4.MD.6

2. What is the closest measure for the angle below?

   A. 25° C. 75°
   B. 55° D. 95°

   4.MD.6

3. How many times larger is a yard than a foot?

   A. 1
   B. 3
   C. 6
   D. 12

   4.MD.1

4. What is the measure of the smaller angle formed by a capital letter L?

   A. 35° C. 75°
   B. 60° D. 90°

   4.MD.6

5. Using the figure below, Stacey started at the top and then made a $\frac{1}{2}$ turn to the bottom. How many degrees did Stacey turn?

   Top

   Left ← → Right

   Bottom

   A. 30°
   B. 60°
   C. 90°
   D. 180°

   4.MD.6

TIP of the DAY

Sometimes the rays of an angle are not long enough to measure on a protractor so we need to make the best choice about its measure.

1. What is another way to write $\frac{8}{5}$?

   A. $\frac{1}{5} + \frac{5}{5} - \frac{2}{5}$

   B. $\frac{2}{5} + \frac{3}{5} + \frac{1}{5}$

   C. $\frac{3}{5} + \frac{3}{5} - \frac{2}{5}$

   D. $\frac{3}{5} + \frac{6}{5} - \frac{1}{5}$

   4.NF.3

Use the figure below to answer questions 2–4.

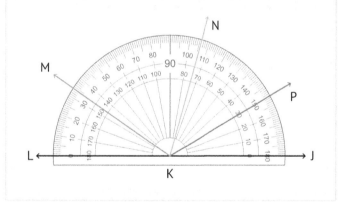

2. How many one-degree angles are in Angle LKM?

   A. 34
   B. 101
   C. 106
   D. 147

   4.MD.6

3. What is the measure of Angle NKJ?

   A. 34°
   B. 74°
   C. 106°
   D. 147°

   4.MD.6

4. What is the measure of Angle LKP?

   A. 30°
   B. 90°
   C. 150°
   D. 270°

   4.MD.6

5. Use the table below to answer the question that follows.

Item	Price
Shoes	71
Jacket	119
Hair band	12

   Pippa went shopping and purchased 3 pairs of shoes, 2 jackets and 5 hair bands. How much money did she spend?

   A. $202
   B. $511
   C. $571
   D. $630

   4.OA.3

TIP of the DAY

Don't forget there are 360° in a circle.

Use the figure below to answer questions 1–4.

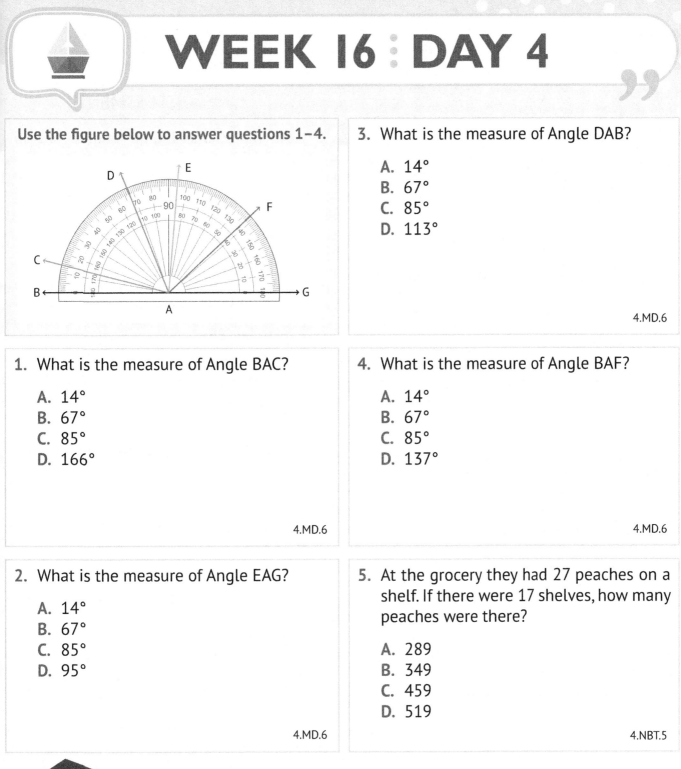

1. What is the measure of Angle BAC?

A. 14°
B. 67°
C. 85°
D. 166°

4.MD.6

2. What is the measure of Angle EAG?

A. 14°
B. 67°
C. 85°
D. 95°

4.MD.6

3. What is the measure of Angle DAB?

A. 14°
B. 67°
C. 85°
D. 113°

4.MD.6

4. What is the measure of Angle BAF?

A. 14°
B. 67°
C. 85°
D. 137°

4.MD.6

5. At the grocery they had 27 peaches on a shelf. If there were 17 shelves, how many peaches were there?

A. 289
B. 349
C. 459
D. 519

4.NBT.5

TIP of the DAY

Remember that every angle can be made up of many one-degree angles.

WEEK 16 : DAY 5

ASSESSMENT

1.

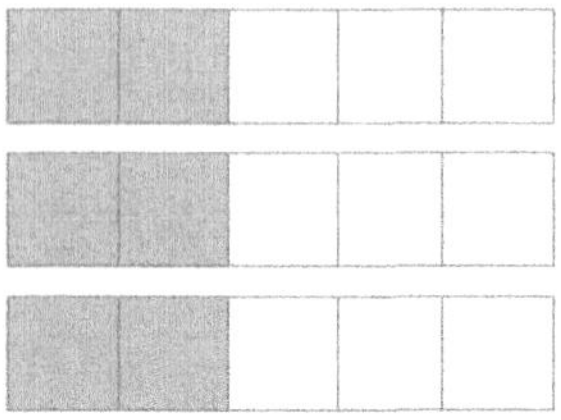

Which equation is modeled by the figure above?

A. $\frac{2}{5} \times 3 = \frac{6}{5}$

B. $\frac{1}{5} \times 6 = \frac{15}{5}$

C. $\frac{2}{3} \times 3 = \frac{6}{3}$

D. $\frac{2}{5} \times 6 = \frac{12}{5}$

4.NF.4

Use the figure below to answer questions 2–5.

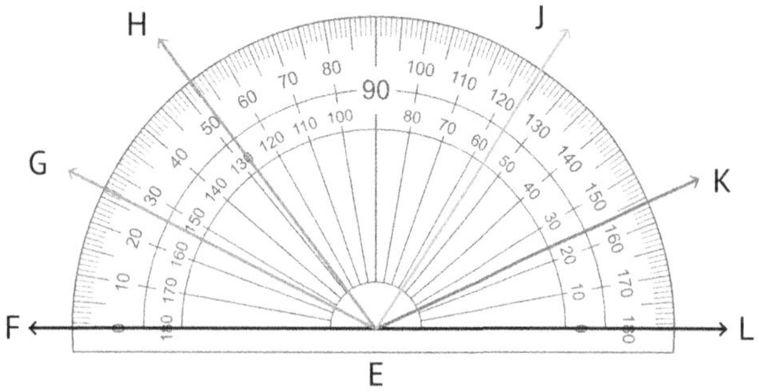

2. How many one-degree angles are in Angle FEJ?

A. 56
B. 78
C. 124
D. 156

4.MD.6

3. Which angle is 152°?

A. Angle KEF
B. Angle LEH
C. Angle FEG
D. Angle LEG

4.MD.6

4. What is the measure of Angle LEF?

A. 45°
B. 90°
C. 135°
D. 180°

4.MD.6

5. How many one-degree angles are in Angle JEL?

A. 56
B. 78
C. 124
D. 156

4.MD.6

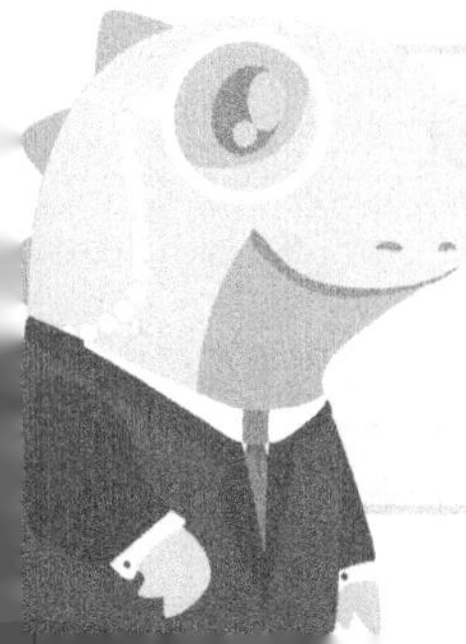

DAY 6
Challenge question

Using the figure above, find the measure of Angle JEG.

4.MD.6

ARGOPREP.COM

VIDEO
EXPLANATIONS

Week 17 works with multiple angles to add them up or separate them. You'll use this information to find missing angle measures.

**You can find detailed video explanations of each problem in the book by visiting:
ArgoPrep.com**

1. Angle RPQ is 32° and Angle NPQ is 51°. What is the measure of Angle RPN?

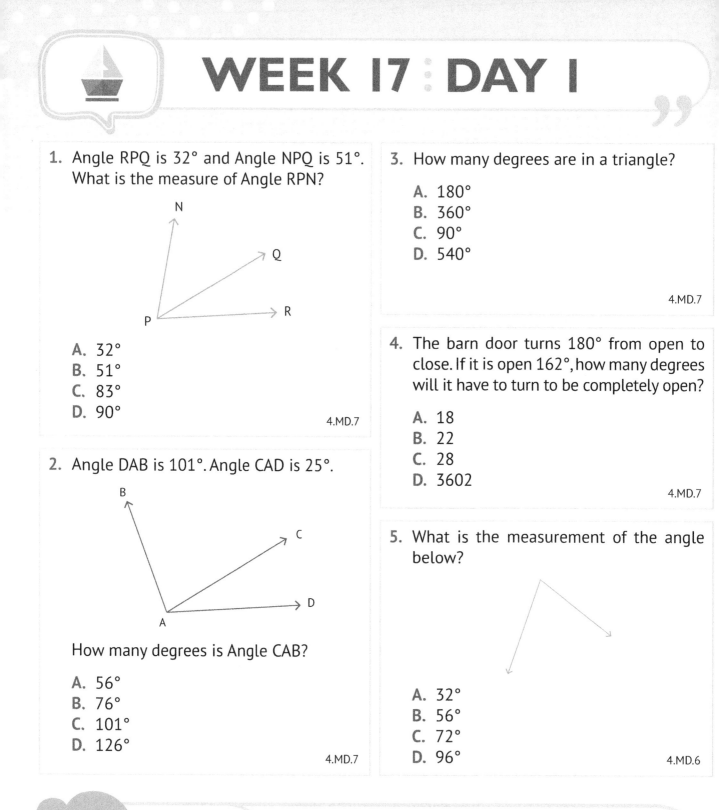

A. 32°
B. 51°
C. 83°
D. 90°

4.MD.7

2. Angle DAB is 101°. Angle CAD is 25°.

How many degrees is Angle CAB?

A. 56°
B. 76°
C. 101°
D. 126°

4.MD.7

3. How many degrees are in a triangle?

A. 180°
B. 360°
C. 90°
D. 540°

4.MD.7

4. The barn door turns 180° from open to close. If it is open 162°, how many degrees will it have to turn to be completely open?

A. 18
B. 22
C. 28
D. 3602

4.MD.7

5. What is the measurement of the angle below?

A. 32°
B. 56°
C. 72°
D. 96°

4.MD.6

TIP *of the* **DAY**

If two angles are combined to form a larger angle, the measure of the larger is the sum of the two original angles.

1. If the hands on the clock show 9:00, how many degrees does the minute hand move until it is 9:30?

   A. 30°
   B. 90°
   C. 180°
   D. 270°

   4.MD.7

Use the figure below to answer questions 2–3.

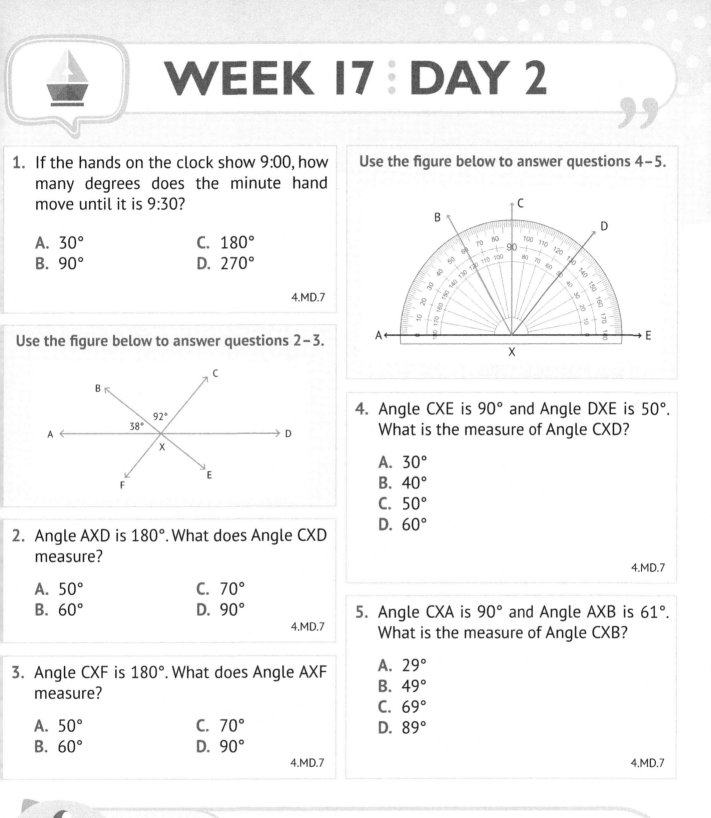

2. Angle AXD is 180°. What does Angle CXD measure?

   A. 50°
   B. 60°
   C. 70°
   D. 90°

   4.MD.7

3. Angle CXF is 180°. What does Angle AXF measure?

   A. 50°
   B. 60°
   C. 70°
   D. 90°

   4.MD.7

Use the figure below to answer questions 4–5.

4. Angle CXE is 90° and Angle DXE is 50°. What is the measure of Angle CXD?

   A. 30°
   B. 40°
   C. 50°
   D. 60°

   4.MD.7

5. Angle CXA is 90° and Angle AXB is 61°. What is the measure of Angle CXB?

   A. 29°
   B. 49°
   C. 69°
   D. 89°

   4.MD.7

TIP of the DAY

Have you noticed that a straight line measures 180°?

Use the figure below to answer questions 1–2.

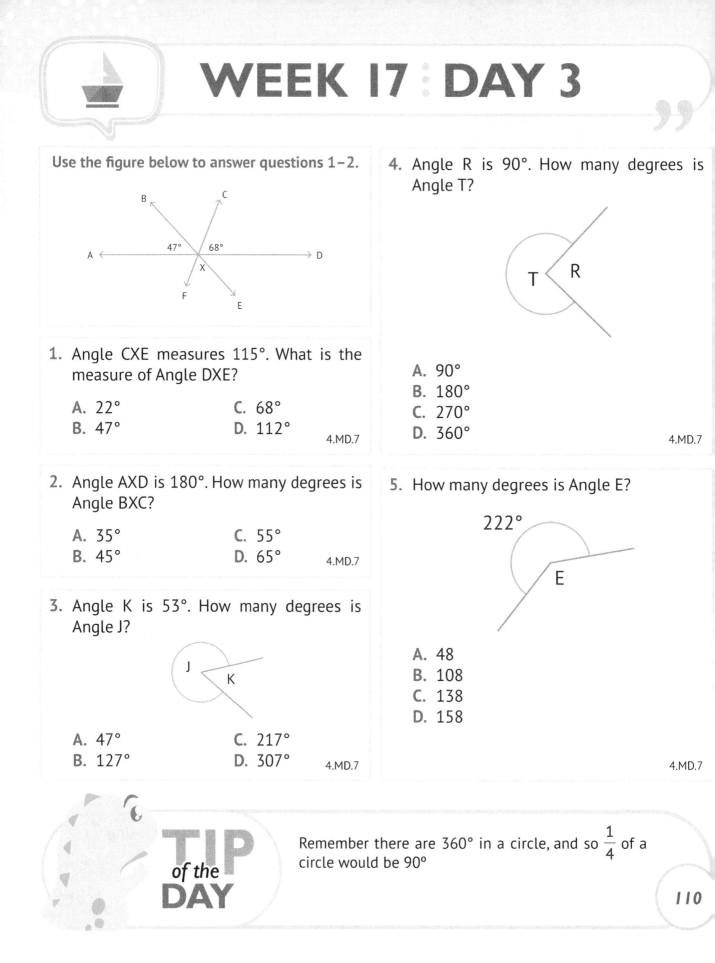

1. Angle CXE measures 115°. What is the measure of Angle DXE?

A. 22° C. 68°

B. 47° D. 112°

4.MD.7

2. Angle AXD is 180°. How many degrees is Angle BXC?

A. 35° C. 55°

B. 45° D. 65°

4.MD.7

3. Angle K is 53°. How many degrees is Angle J?

A. 47° C. 217°

B. 127° D. 307°

4.MD.7

4. Angle R is 90°. How many degrees is Angle T?

A. 90°

B. 180°

C. 270°

D. 360°

4.MD.7

5. How many degrees is Angle E?

222°

A. 48

B. 108

C. 138

D. 158

4.MD.7

TIP of the DAY

Remember there are 360° in a circle, and so $\frac{1}{4}$ of a circle would be 90°

Use the figure below to answer questions 1–3.

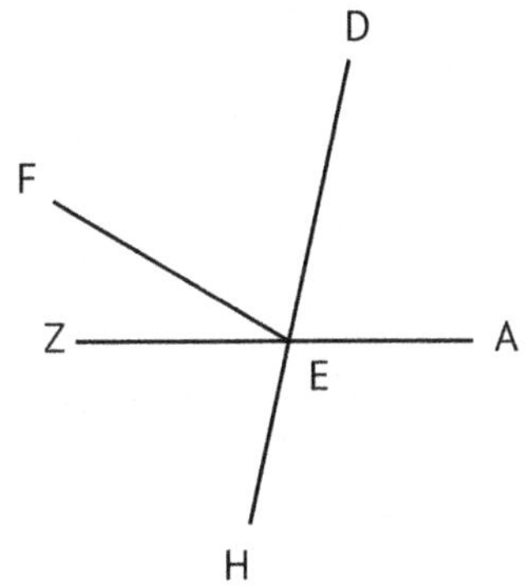

D
F
Z — E — A
H

1. If Angle ZEF is 46° and Angle ZED is 99°, what is Angle DEF?

A. 44°
B. 46°
C. 51°
D. 53°

4.MD.7

2. If Angle DEH is 180° and Angle AEH is 103°, what is the measure of Angle DEA?

A. 13°
B. 46°
C. 77°
D. 96°

4.MD.7

3. If Angle FEH is 121° and Angle ZEH is 73°, what is the measure of Angle FEZ?

A. 34°
B. 48°
C. 149°
D. 194°

4.MD.7

4. Which one of the statements below is true?

A. 4,600 > 4,598
B. 2 hundreds + 4 tens < 14 tens
C. 5 × 1000 + 6 × 1 = 5 × 100 + 6 × 10
D. 1270 × 4 < 89 × 21

4.NBT.2

5. If Angle ABC + Angle CBD = 180° and Angle ABC is 94°, what is the measure of Angle CBD?

A. 4°
B. 76°
C. 86°
D. 274°

4.MD.7

TIP of the DAY

When adding or subtracting to find angle measures, be sure to complete the addition and subtraction very carefully to avoid errors.

WEEK 17 : DAY 5

1. The outside angle is 222°. How many degrees is Angle E?

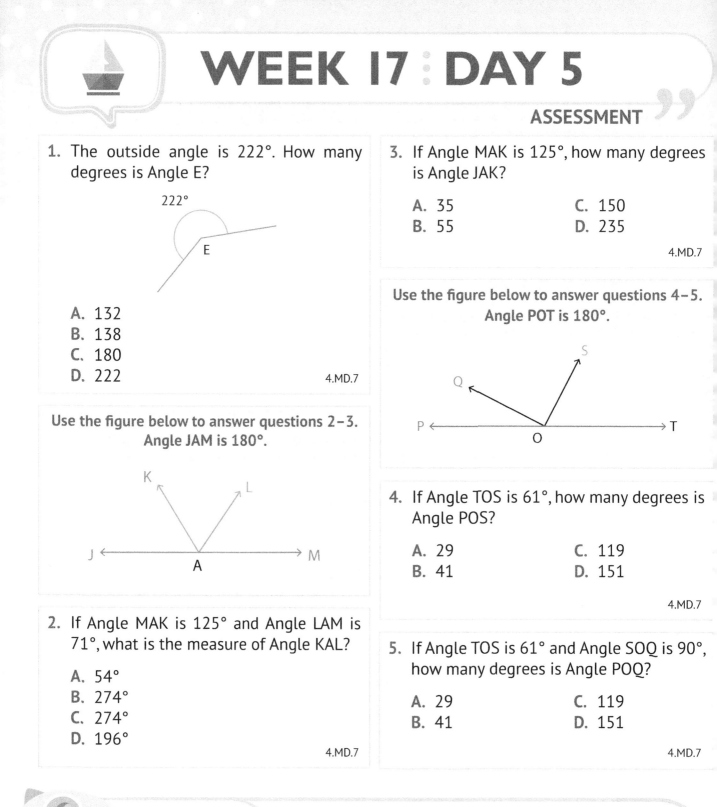

222°

E

A. 132
B. 138
C. 180
D. 222

4.MD.7

Use the figure below to answer questions 2–3.
Angle JAM is 180°.

K   L

J ←————————→ M
          A

2. If Angle MAK is 125° and Angle LAM is 71°, what is the measure of Angle KAL?

A. 54°
B. 274°
C. 274°
D. 196°

4.MD.7

3. If Angle MAK is 125°, how many degrees is Angle JAK?

A. 35   C. 150
B. 55   D. 235

4.MD.7

Use the figure below to answer questions 4–5.
Angle POT is 180°.

S

Q

P ←————————→ T
          O

4. If Angle TOS is 61°, how many degrees is Angle POS?

A. 29   C. 119
B. 41   D. 151

4.MD.7

5. If Angle TOS is 61° and Angle SOQ is 90°, how many degrees is Angle POQ?

A. 29   C. 119
B. 41   D. 151

4.MD.7

DAY 6
Challenge question

Find a triangle. Measure the three angles in that triangle and add together their angles. Do the same thing to a different triangle. What do you notice?

4.MD.7

112

WEEK 18

VIDEO EXPLANATIONS ▶

ARGOPREP.COM

Angles aren't the only geometry you'll be able to practice. This week you'll also have a chance to work with specific angles (right, acute, obtuse) and certain types of lines such as parallel and perpendicular lines.

You can find detailed video explanations of each problem in the book by visiting:
ArgoPrep.com

1. What type of angles do perpendicular lines make?

   A. acute
   B. obtuse
   C. right
   D. parallel

   4.G.1

Use the figures below to answer questions 2–5.

   A.   B.   C.   D.

2. Which shape has exactly TWO sets of parallel lines?

   A. A
   B. B
   C. C
   D. D

   4.G.1

3. Which shape has one right angle?

   A. A
   B. B
   C. C
   D. D

   4.G.1

4. Which shape has ZERO obtuse angles?

   A. A
   B. B
   C. C
   D. D

   4.G.1

5. Which 2 shapes have exactly TWO acute angles?

   A. A and B
   B. B and C
   C. C and D
   D. D and A

   4.G.1

6. What number goes in the blank to make the sentence true?

   The number 110 is _____ times greater than the number 10.

   A. 9
   B. 10
   C. 11
   D. 12

   4.OA.1

TIP of the DAY

Remember that right angles measure 90°.

114

Use the figure below to answer questions 1–5.

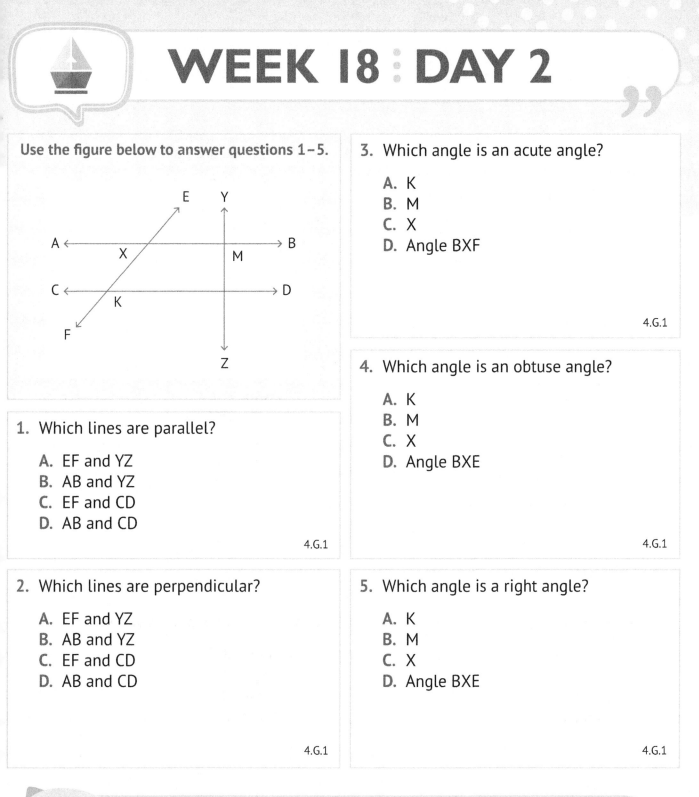

1. Which lines are parallel?

A. EF and YZ
B. AB and YZ
C. EF and CD
D. AB and CD

4.G.1

2. Which lines are perpendicular?

A. EF and YZ
B. AB and YZ
C. EF and CD
D. AB and CD

4.G.1

3. Which angle is an acute angle?

A. K
B. M
C. X
D. Angle BXF

4.G.1

4. Which angle is an obtuse angle?

A. K
B. M
C. X
D. Angle BXE

4.G.1

5. Which angle is a right angle?

A. K
B. M
C. X
D. Angle BXE

4.G.1

1. The trip to Detroit was 9 times as far as the trip to Chicago. Which equation can be used to find the distance to Detroit if D represents the distance to Detroit and C represents the distance to Chicago?

   A. $C = 9 + D$
   B. $C = 9 \times D$
   C. $D = 9 + C$
   D. $D = 9 \times C$

   4.OA.2

Use the figure below to answer questions 2–5.

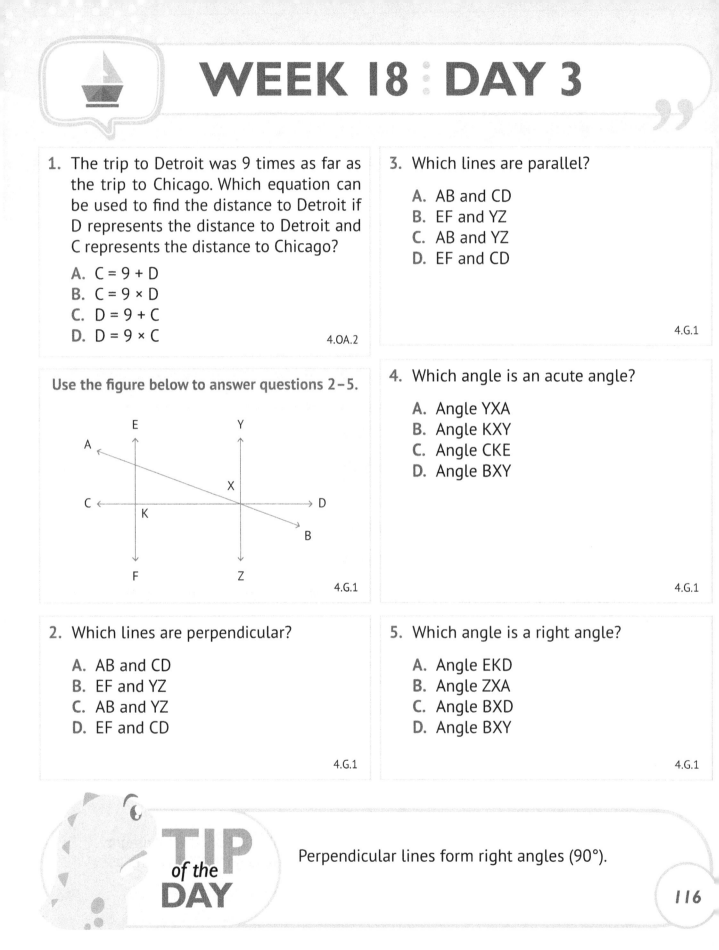

4.G.1

2. Which lines are perpendicular?

   A. AB and CD
   B. EF and YZ
   C. AB and YZ
   D. EF and CD

   4.G.1

3. Which lines are parallel?

   A. AB and CD
   B. EF and YZ
   C. AB and YZ
   D. EF and CD

   4.G.1

4. Which angle is an acute angle?

   A. Angle YXA
   B. Angle KXY
   C. Angle CKE
   D. Angle BXY

   4.G.1

5. Which angle is a right angle?

   A. Angle EKD
   B. Angle ZXA
   C. Angle BXD
   D. Angle BXY

   4.G.1

TIP of the DAY

Perpendicular lines form right angles (90°).

1. What is $3\frac{3}{4} + 11\frac{3}{4}$?

   A. 8

   B. 14

   C. $15\frac{1}{2}$

   D. $16\frac{1}{4}$

   4.NF.3

Use the figure below to answer questions 2-5.

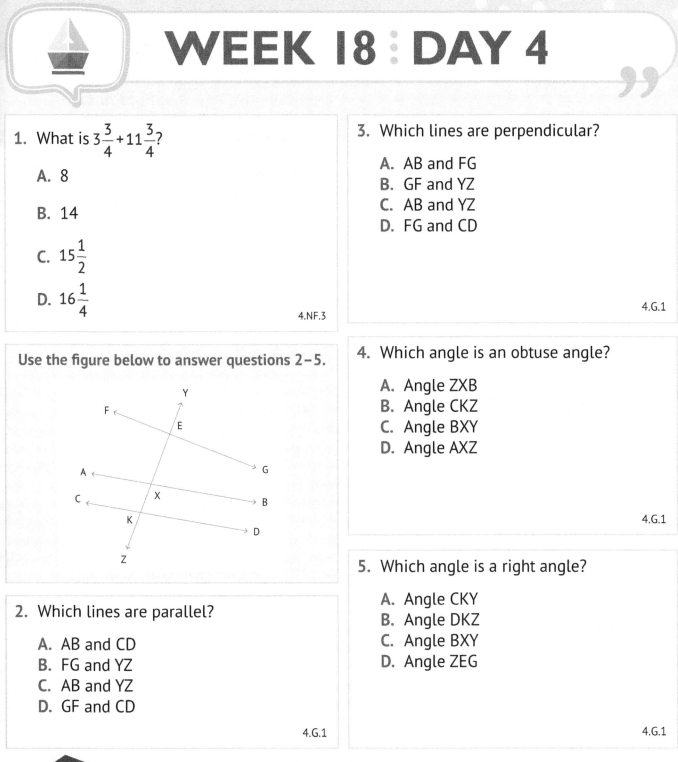

2. Which lines are parallel?

   A. AB and CD
   B. FG and YZ
   C. AB and YZ
   D. GF and CD

   4.G.1

3. Which lines are perpendicular?

   A. AB and FG
   B. GF and YZ
   C. AB and YZ
   D. FG and CD

   4.G.1

4. Which angle is an obtuse angle?

   A. Angle ZXB
   B. Angle CKZ
   C. Angle BXY
   D. Angle AXZ

   4.G.1

5. Which angle is a right angle?

   A. Angle CKY
   B. Angle DKZ
   C. Angle BXY
   D. Angle ZEG

   4.G.1

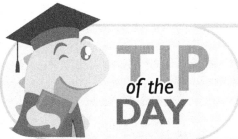

TIP *of the* **DAY**

Parallel lines will never intersect, even if you draw the lines forever in either direction.

WEEK 18 : DAY 5

Use the figures below to answer questions 1–5.

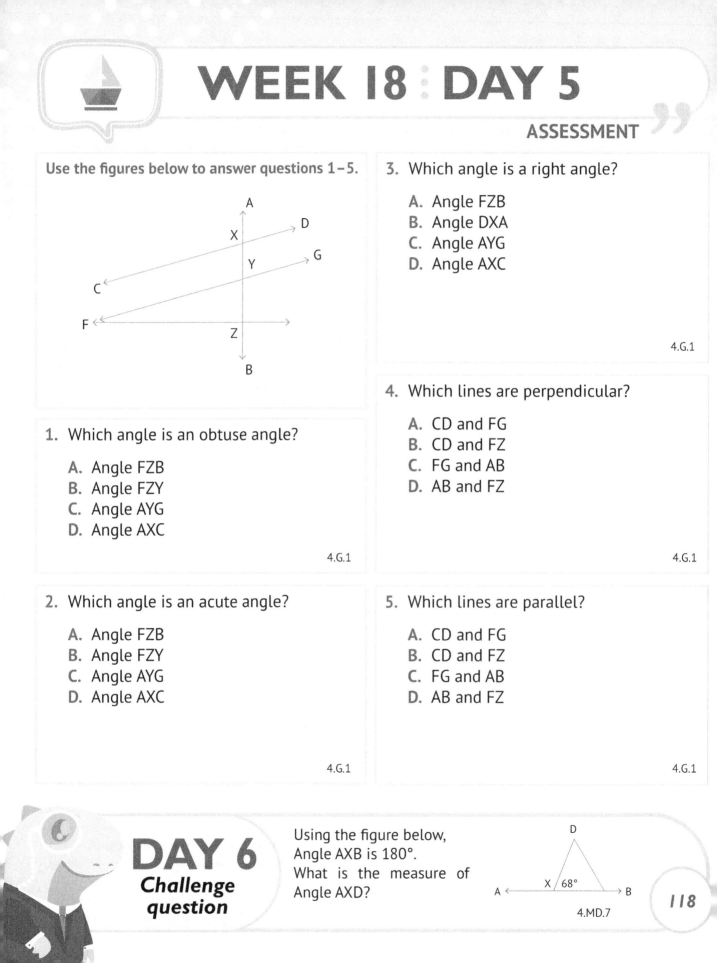

1. Which angle is an obtuse angle?

A. Angle FZB
B. Angle FZY
C. Angle AYG
D. Angle AXC

4.G.1

2. Which angle is an acute angle?

A. Angle FZB
B. Angle FZY
C. Angle AYG
D. Angle AXC

4.G.1

3. Which angle is a right angle?

A. Angle FZB
B. Angle DXA
C. Angle AYG
D. Angle AXC

4.G.1

4. Which lines are perpendicular?

A. CD and FG
B. CD and FZ
C. FG and AB
D. AB and FZ

4.G.1

5. Which lines are parallel?

A. CD and FG
B. CD and FZ
C. FG and AB
D. AB and FZ

4.G.1

DAY 6
Challenge question

Using the figure below, Angle AXB is 180°. What is the measure of Angle AXD?

4.MD.7

118

WEEK 19

VIDEO EXPLANATIONS ▶ ARGOPREP.COM

This week you'll see geometric shapes that have examples of the angles and types of lines that you've worked with in the previous couple of weeks. You'll also find and draw right triangles.

You can find detailed video explanations of each problem in the book by visiting:
ArgoPrep.com

Use the figures below to answer questions 1–4.

A.　　　B.　　　C.　　　D.

3. Which figure has exactly 3 acute angles?

A. A
B. B
C. C
D. D

4.G.2

1. Which figure has a right angle?

A. A
B. B
C. C
D. D

4.G.2

4. Which figure has one pair of parallel lines?

A. A
B. B
C. C
D. D

4.G.2

2. Which figure has 2 right angles?

A. A
B. B
C. C
D. D

4.G.2

5. Mindy ran $\frac{7}{10}$ of a kilometer. Which expression equals $\frac{7}{10}$?

A. 710
B. 7.0
C. 0.07
D. 0.70

4.NF.6

TIP of the DAY

Remember that a right angle measures 90°. An angle that is less than 90° is an acute angle and an angle that measures larger than 90° is an obtuse angle.

120

WEEK 19 : DAY 2

Use the figures below to answer questions 1–2.

A.   B.   C.   D.

1. Which figure does NOT have a right angle?

A. A
B. B
C. C
D. D

4.G.2

2. Which figure has EXACTLY 4 right angles?

A. A
B. B
C. C
D. D

4.G.2

3. What is 4986 divided by 8?

A. 623 r 2
B. 622 r 6
C. 623 r 1
D. 623 r 6

4.NBT.6

4. Which figure appears to be a right triangle?

A.   B.   C.   D.

4.G.2

5. Which fraction is NOT equivalent to $\frac{2}{3}$?

A. $\frac{15}{21}$

B. $\frac{10}{15}$

C. $\frac{12}{18}$

D. $\frac{24}{36}$

4NF.1

Use the figures below to answer questions 1–3.

A.   B.   C.   D.

1. Which figure has two pairs of parallel lines?

A. A
B. B
C. C
D. D

4.G.2

2. Which figure has a right angle?

A. A
B. B
C. C
D. D

4.G.2

3. Which 2 figures have exactly one pair of parallel lines?

A. A and D
B. B and C
C. A and C
D. D and B

4.G.2

Use the figures below to answer questions 4–5.

A.   B.   C.   D.

4. Which figure has a right angle?

A. A
B. B
C. C
D. D

4.G.2

5. Which figure has exactly 2 pairs of parallel lines?

A. A   C. C
B. B   D. D

4.G.2

TIP of the DAY

Don't forget what is special about right angles, acute angles and obtuse angles.

Use the figures below to answer questions 1–2.

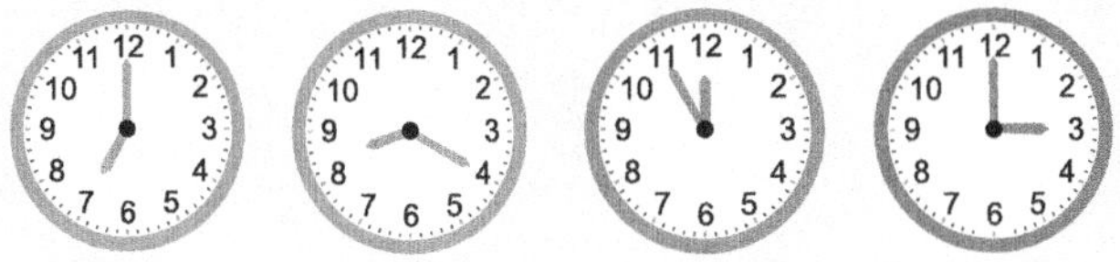

A.   B.   C.   D.

1. Which clock shows a right angle?

A. A
B. B
C. C
D. D

4.G.2

2. Which clock shows an acute angle?

A. A
B. B
C. C
D. D

4.G.2

3. Which number set below contains ONLY composite numbers?

A. 4, 15, 26, 51
B. 16, 25, 47, 64
C. 21, 29, 34, 71
D. 23, 38, 40, 51

4.OA.4

4. Which figure below is NOT a right triangle?

A.   B.   C.   D.

4.G.2

5. Which of the following shapes has two pairs of parallel lines and all right angles?

A. right triangle
B. circle
C. rectangle
D. trapezoid

4.G.2

TIP of the DAY

When you take the next assessment, make sure you understand what each of the terms means.

ASSESSMENT

Use the figures below to answer questions 1–2.

A.   B.   C.   D.

Use the figures below to answer questions 3–5.

A.   B.   C.   D.

1. Which pair of lines is perpendicular?

   A. A
   B. B
   C. C
   D. D

   4.G.2

2. Which pair of lines is parallel?

   A. A
   B. B
   C. C
   D. D

   4.G.2

3. Which figure has exactly ONE right angle?

   A. A
   B. B
   C. C
   D. D

   4.G.2

4. Which figure has TWO pairs of parallel lines?

   A. A
   B. B
   C. C
   D. D

   4.G.2

5. Which figures have ZERO parallel lines?

   A. A and B
   B. C and D
   C. B and C
   D. A and D

   4.G.2

DAY 6
Challenge question

What shape has 2 sets of parallel lines and zero right angles?

4.G.2

Using the geometric shapes from last week, we'll find lines of symmetry for them. Lines of symmetry are lines that perfectly divide a shape in half so that there are mirror images on either side of that line.

You can find detailed video explanations of each problem in the book by visiting:
ArgoPrep.com

Use the figures below to answer questions 1–4.

A.   B.   C.   D.

1. Which figure appears to have exactly 2 lines of symmetry?

A. A
B. B
C. C
D. D

4.G.3

2. Which figures appear to have exactly 1 line of symmetry?

A. A and B
B. C and D
C. A and C
D. B and D

4.G.3

3. Which figure appears to have zero lines of symmetry?

A. A
B. B
C. C
D. D

4.G.3

4. Which figure has exactly one pair of parallel lines?

A. A
B. B
C. C
D. D

4.G.2

5. Which number sentence below is true?

A. $\frac{1}{2} > \frac{2}{3}$

B. $\frac{1}{4} < \frac{3}{12}$

C. $\frac{7}{8} > \frac{4}{5}$

D. $\frac{4}{5} = \frac{24}{28}$

4.NF.2

TIP of the DAY

Symmetry means that one side looks like the mirror image of the other side, if the figure were folded in half.

Use the letters below to answer questions 1-2.

H I G T

1. Which letter has ZERO lines of symmetry?

   A. H
   B. I
   C. G
   D. T

   4.G.3

2. Which letter has EXACTLY 1 line of symmetry?

   A. H
   B. I
   C. G
   D. T

   4.G.3

3. Which figure has exactly 2 lines of symmetry?

   A. H and G
   B. H and T
   C. H and I
   D. I and G

   4.G.3

Use the figures below to answer questions 3-5.

   A.   B.   C.   D.

4. Which figure has EXACTLY 2 lines of symmetry?

   A. A
   B. B
   C. C
   D. D

   4.G.3

5. Which pair of lines is perpendicular?

   A.   B.   C.   D.

   4.G.2

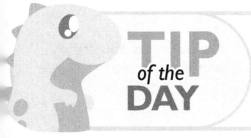

TIP *of the* **DAY**

Symmetry does not mean straight up and down or straight from left to right. Symmetry can be along a diagonal line.

Use the figures below to answer questions 1–2.

A.   B.   C.   D.

1. Which figures do NOT appear to have any lines of symmetry?

A. A and B
B. C and D
C. A and D
D. B and C

4.G.3

2. Which figure appears to have exactly TWO pairs of parallel lines?

A. A
B. B
C. C
D. D

4.G.2

3. Of the following shapes, which one has exactly 4 lines of symmetry?

A. triangle
B. trapezoid
C. square
D. rectangle

4.G.3

Use the figures below to answer questions 4–5.

X O P R

4. Which two letters have exactly TWO lines of symmetry?

A. X and O
B. X and P
C. R and O
D. P and R

4.G.3

5. Which two letters have ZERO lines of symmetry?

A. X and O
B. X and P
C. R and O
D. P and R

4.G.3

TIP of the DAY

You are almost finished with this workbook. You are going to be so prepared for your next math test!

WEEK 20 : DAY 4

Use the figures below to answer questions 1–3.

A.   B.   C.   D.

3. Which 2 figures have only 1 line of symmetry?

A. A and B
B. C and D
C. B and D
D. A and C

4.G.3

1. Which figure has the largest number of symmetry lines?

A. A
B. B
C. C
D. D

4.G.3

4. Which figure below appears to be a right triangle?

A.   B.   C.   D.

4.G.2

2. Which figure has exactly 2 lines of symmetry?

A. A
B. B
C. C
D. D

4.G.3

5. Which of the following letters has 2 lines of symmetry?

A. A
B. B
C. T
D. H

4.G.3

TIP of the DAY

If you get stuck on a problem, see if you can eliminate some answer choices that you know are NOT possible.

WEEK 20 : DAY 5

ASSESSMENT

Use the figures below to answer question 1.

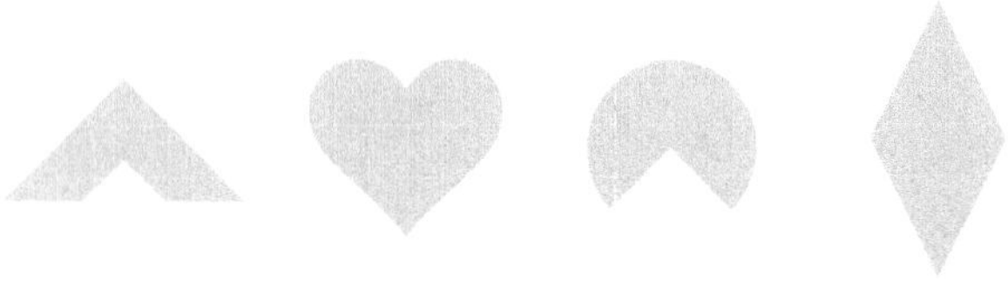

A. B. C. D.

1. Which figure has more than 1 line of symmetry?

   A. A
   B. B
   C. C
   D. D

4.G.3

2. Which of the following letters has ZERO lines of symmetry?

   A. E
   B. W
   C. F
   D. T

4.G.3

Use the figures below to answer questions 3–4.

Q Y E X

3. Which letter has 2 lines of symmetry?

   A. Q
   B. Y
   C. E
   D. X

4.G.3

4. Which letter has ZERO lines of symmetry?

   A. Q
   B. Y
   C. E
   D. X

4.G.3

5. How many lines of symmetry does the figure below have?

   A. 0
   B. 1
   C. 2
   D. 3

4.G.3

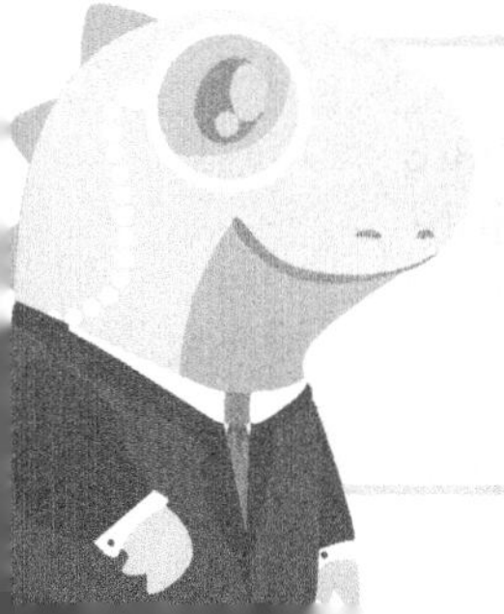

DAY 6
Challenge question

How many lines of symmetry does a circle have?

4.G.3

THE
END

**Great job finishing all 20 weeks!
You should be ready for any test.**

ASSESSMENT

Try this assessment to see how much you've learned - good luck!

ASSESSMENT

1. If 11 × 6 = 66, then which statement is true?

   A. 66 is 11 times greater than 6.
   B. 11 is 6 times greater than 66.
   C. 66 is 11 times less than 6.
   D. 6 is ll times greater than 66.   4.OA.1

2. Mille buys 8 loaves of bread, 12 donuts and 6 bagels. What is the cost of Mille's purchase?

Bakery Item	Price
One Loaf of Bread	$8
Donut	$3
Bagel	$2

   A. $100   C. $112
   B. $102   D. $120
                                          4.OA.3

3. What is the next number in the pattern?
   34, 31, ____, 25

   A. 30   C. 27
   B. 28   D. 26
                                          4.OA.5

4. Which set of numbers has all the factors of 42?

   A. 1, 2, 3, 4, 6, 7, 12, 14, 42
   B. 1, 2, 5, 6, 7, 21, 42
   C. 1, 2, 3, 6, 7, 12, 14, 21, 42
   D. 1, 2, 3, 6, 7, 14, 21, 42
                                          4.OA.4

5. How many times greater is the 8 in 1,826 than the 8 in 983?

   A. 1
   B. 10
   C. 100
   D. 1,000   4.NBT.1

6. Which of the statements is true?

   A. 4 thousands + 6 hundreds + 2 ones > 5 thousands
   B. 8 hundreds + 8 tens + 9 ones < 8 hundreds + 8 tens + 5 ones
   C. 5 thousands + 2 hundreds = 52 hundreds
   D. 3 hundreds + 7 tens + 2 ones > 3 hundreds + 8 tens   4.NBT.2

7. What is $\frac{3}{100} + \frac{8}{10}$?

   A. $\frac{38}{10}$ C. $\frac{83}{10}$

   B. $\frac{38}{100}$ D. $\frac{83}{100}$ 4.NF.5

8. Which ordered pair would complete the table?

Kilometers	Meters
1000	1
3000	3

   A. (2000, 2)   C. (1000, 3)   4.MD.1
   B. (2, 2000)   D. (3, 1000)

134

9. The area of a hallway is 30 ft², if the length is 10 feet, what is the perimeter?

A. 3 feet   C. 26 feet
B. 10 feet   D. 300 feet

4.MD.3

10. The trail is 0.97 of a kilometer long. How long is the trail?

A. $\dfrac{97}{10}$ km   C. $\dfrac{97}{1000}$ km

B. $\dfrac{97}{100}$ km   D. $\dfrac{97}{10,000}$ km

4.NF.6

11. Which statement is true?

A. $13 < 12.98$
B. $152.6 > 152.37$
C. $431.49 = 431.5$
D. $875.03 = 875.30$

4.NF.7

12. There will be 48 people at the party. Each one will eat $\dfrac{3}{4}$ cup of ice cream. Which equation can be used to find out how much ice cream is needed?

A. $48 \times \dfrac{3}{4} = 144$ cups

B. $48 \times \dfrac{3}{4} = 36$ cups

C. $48 \div \dfrac{3}{4} = 36$ cups

D. $48 \div \dfrac{3}{4} = 144$ cups

4.NF.4

13. What is $14\dfrac{2}{5} - 11\dfrac{3}{5}$?

A. $3\dfrac{1}{5}$ C. $2\dfrac{1}{5}$

B. $3\dfrac{4}{5}$ D. $2\dfrac{4}{5}$

4.NF.3

14. Which number sentence is true?

A. $\dfrac{3}{12} = \dfrac{1}{4}$ C. $\dfrac{1}{4} > \dfrac{1}{3}$

B. $\dfrac{3}{4} > \dfrac{1}{1}$ D. $\dfrac{7}{8} < \dfrac{5}{6}$

4.NF.2

15. What is the product of 4,117 and 9?

A. 4,128   C. 36,863
B. 36,503   D. 37,053

4.NBT.5

16. What is 156,398,017 rounded to the nearest ten thousand?

A. 156,398,000
B. 156,390,000
C. 156,400,000
D. 156,000,000

4.NBT.3

17. What is the quotient of 3562 and 7?

A. 58 r 6
B. 508 r 6
C. 509 r 1
D. 509 r4

4.NBT.6

18. Which expression is equivalent to $\frac{10}{7}$?

A. $\frac{1}{7} + \frac{5}{7} + \frac{3}{7} - \frac{2}{7}$

B. $\frac{4}{7} + \frac{6}{7} - \frac{1}{7} + \frac{2}{7}$

C. $\frac{2}{7} + \frac{5}{7} + \frac{4}{7} - \frac{1}{7}$

D. $\frac{6}{7} + \frac{4}{7} - \frac{5}{7} - \frac{1}{7}$

4.NF.3

19. Use the models below to find the true statement.

A. $\frac{3}{6} = \frac{2}{3}$

C. $\frac{6}{4} = \frac{2}{1}$

B. $\frac{4}{6} = \frac{1}{3}$

D. $\frac{4}{6} = \frac{2}{3}$

4.NF.1

20. Marvin read $\frac{3}{8}$ of his book on Sunday and $\frac{2}{8}$ on Monday. How much of his book is left to read?

A. $\frac{1}{8}$

C. $\frac{3}{8}$

B. $\frac{2}{8}$

D. $\frac{5}{8}$

4.NF.3

21. Krista ran 5 kilometers and Jamey ran 5000 meters. Who ran the furthest?

A. They ran the same distance because 5 km = 5000 m.
B. Krista ran further because kilometers are larger than meters.
C. Jamey ran further because 5000 is larger than 5.
D. Jamey ran further because she ran 5000 m, which is longer than 5 km.

4.MD.2

22. How many one-degree angles are in an angle that measures 103 degrees?

A. 13   C. 77

B. 103   D. 167   4.MD.5

Use the figure below to answer questions 23–24.

A.   B.   C.   D.

23. Which of the figures has no parallel lines?

A.   B.   C.   D.

4.G.2

24. Which of the figures has exactly ONE line of symmetry?

4.G.3

A.   B.   C.   D.

25. Use the figure below to answer the question.

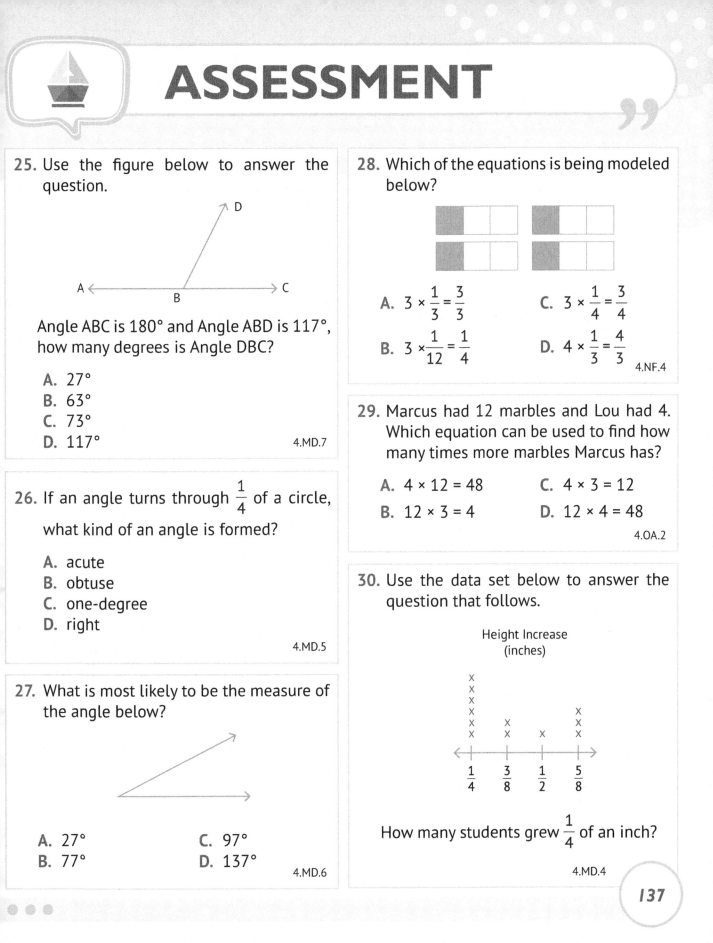

Angle ABC is 180° and Angle ABD is 117°, how many degrees is Angle DBC?

A. 27°

B. 63°

C. 73°

D. 117°

4.MD.7

26. If an angle turns through $\frac{1}{4}$ of a circle, what kind of an angle is formed?

A. acute

B. obtuse

C. one-degree

D. right

4.MD.5

27. What is most likely to be the measure of the angle below?

A. 27°   C. 97°

B. 77°   D. 137°

4.MD.6

28. Which of the equations is being modeled below?

A. $3 \times \frac{1}{3} = \frac{3}{3}$ C. $3 \times \frac{1}{4} = \frac{3}{4}$

B. $3 \times \frac{1}{12} = \frac{1}{4}$ D. $4 \times \frac{1}{3} = \frac{4}{3}$

4.NF.4

29. Marcus had 12 marbles and Lou had 4. Which equation can be used to find how many times more marbles Marcus has?

A. 4 × 12 = 48   C. 4 × 3 = 12

B. 12 × 3 = 4   D. 12 × 4 = 48

4.OA.2

30. Use the data set below to answer the question that follows.

Height Increase
(inches)

How many students grew $\frac{1}{4}$ of an inch?

4.MD.4

137

31. Glen wants to fence his yard. He knows it has an area of 450 square yards and is 15 yards wide. How much fencing would he need?

4.MD.3

32. Each cabin needs $\frac{3}{5}$ acre of land. If there are 12 cabins, how much land is needed?

4.NF.4

33. List all of the factors of 24.

_____

4.OA.4

34. What numbers are missing in the pattern below?

____, 37, 40, 43, ____, 49

4.OA.5

35. Write four hundred three thousand, six hundred, twenty-nine in expanded form.

_____

4.NBT.2

36. Write a number sentence using $\frac{4}{5}$ and $\frac{9}{10}$. Use a model to prove your answer.

_____

4.NF.2

37. Angle AXD is 180°. Write a subtraction equation to find the measure of Angle AXB.

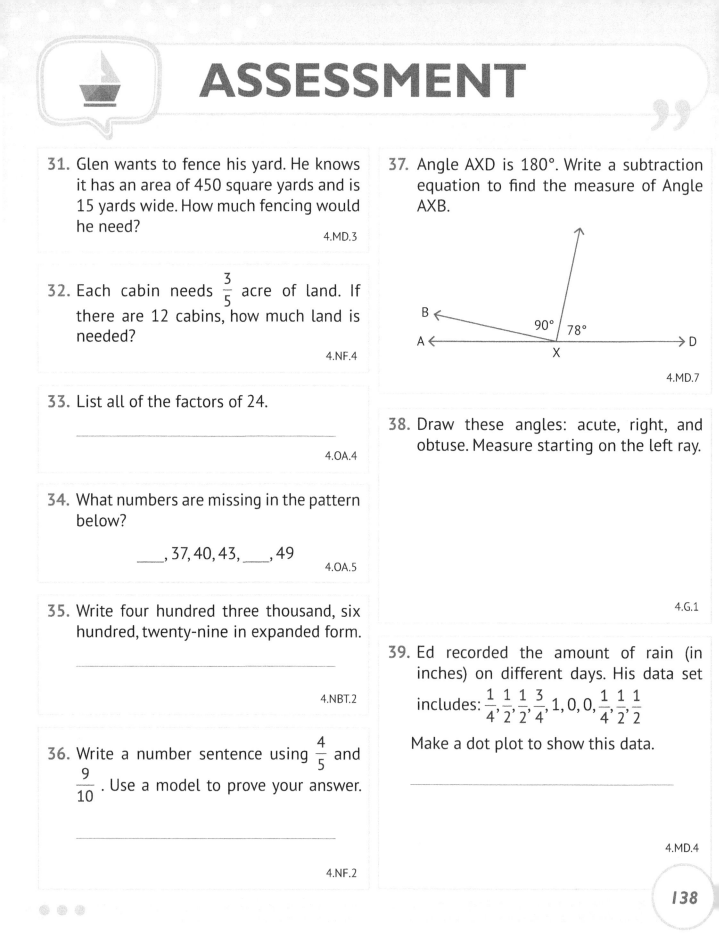

4.MD.7

38. Draw these angles: acute, right, and obtuse. Measure starting on the left ray.

4.G.1

39. Ed recorded the amount of rain (in inches) on different days. His data set includes: $\frac{1}{4}, \frac{1}{2}, \frac{1}{2}, \frac{3}{4}, 1, 0, 0, \frac{1}{4}, \frac{1}{2}, \frac{1}{2}$

Make a dot plot to show this data.

_____

4.MD.4

ASSESSMENT

40. Ralph has 1 snake that is 3 feet and another snake that is 8 feet. How long is each snake in inches?

_____

4.MD.1

41. The chart below shows how many yards Susan walked on some days. How many feet did she walk?

Day	Yards Walked
Monday	954
Wednesday	785
Friday	811

4.MD.2

42. What must each angle have to be considered an angle?

_____

4.MD.5

43. What are the lines of symmetry for the following figures?

_____

4.G.3

44. Tillie made peach tea by combining $5\frac{1}{5}$ gallons of tea with $1\frac{4}{5}$ gallons of Peach-Ade. Then she drank $\frac{1}{5}$ gallon to taste it. How much peach tea did she have after tasting?

_____

4.NF.3

45. Each sandwich needs $\frac{1}{8}$ of a pound of salami, $\frac{2}{8}$ pound of ham and $\frac{3}{8}$ pound of roast beef. How much meat is needed for 10 sandwiches?

_____

4.NF.4

ANSWER KEY

WEEK 1

DAY 1	DAY 2	DAY 3	DAY 4	DAY 5
1. A	1. C	1. B	1. D	1. A
2. C	2. A	2. B	2. C	2. D
3. B	3. C	3. A	3. D	3. A
4. D	4. D	4. D	4. A	4. B
5. D	5. A	5. B	5. A	5. C
6. B	6. D	6. C	6. B	6. B

WEEK 2

DAY 1	DAY 2	DAY 3	DAY 4	DAY 5
1. A	1. A	1. B	1. B	1. D
2. D	2. C	2. C	2. C	2. C
3. C	3. C	3. C	3. D	3. B
4. A	4. B	4. B	4. B	4. D
5. B	5. D	5. D	5. B	5. A
6. D		6. D		6. D

WEEK 3

DAY 1	DAY 2	DAY 3	DAY 4	DAY 5
1. B	1. C	1. B	1. B	1. D
2. C	2. B	2. C	2. A	2. C
3. C	3. D	3. D	3. C	3. C
4. D	4. D	4. B	4. B	4. B
5. C	5. A	5. D	5. A	5. A
6. A	6. A	6. B	6. D	6. D

WEEK 4

DAY 1	DAY 2	DAY 3	DAY 4	DAY 5
1. B	1. C	1. C	1. D	1. A
2. A	2. A	2. A	2. B	2. B
3. C	3. B	3. B	3. A	3. C
4. A	4. C	4. D	4. C	4. C
5. D	5. D	5. A	5. A	5. B
6. C	6. C	6. D		6. B

WEEK 5

DAY 1	DAY 2	DAY 3	DAY 4	DAY 5
1. A	1. B	1. D	1. D	1. C
2. D	2. A	2. B	2. C	2. D
3. B	3. D	3. B	3. D	3. A
4. D	4. C	4. C	4. A	4. B
5. A	5. B	5. A	5. B	5. D
6. D	6. D	6. C	6. D	6. D

WEEK 6

DAY 1	DAY 2	DAY 3	DAY 4	DAY 5
1. C	1. A	1. D	1. A	1. C
2. D	2. C	2. C	2. B	2. C
3. A	3. B	3. A	3. D	3. D
4. D	4. D	4. A	4. D	4. A
5. B	5. C	5. D	5. C	5. B
6. B	6. A	6. B	6. A	6. A

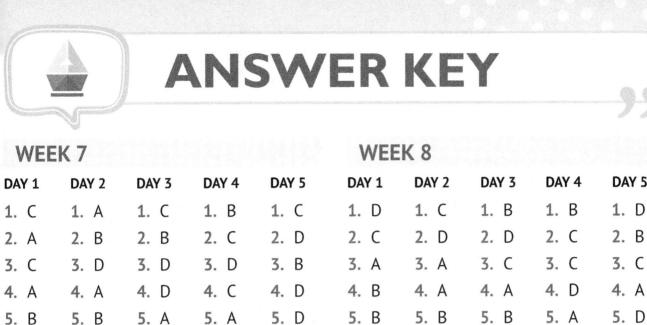

ANSWER KEY

WEEK 7

DAY 1	DAY 2	DAY 3	DAY 4	DAY 5
1. C	1. A	1. C	1. B	1. C
2. A	2. B	2. B	2. C	2. D
3. C	3. D	3. D	3. D	3. B
4. A	4. A	4. D	4. C	4. D
5. B	5. B	5. A	5. A	5. D
6. D	6. A	6. B	6. D	6. C

WEEK 8

DAY 1	DAY 2	DAY 3	DAY 4	DAY 5
1. D	1. C	1. B	1. B	1. D
2. C	2. D	2. D	2. C	2. B
3. A	3. A	3. C	3. C	3. C
4. B	4. A	4. A	4. D	4. A
5. B	5. B	5. B	5. A	5. D
6. A	6. C	6. C		6. D

WEEK 9

DAY 1	DAY 2	DAY 3	DAY 4	DAY 5
1. A	1. B	1. C	1. B	1. C
2. C	2. B	2. A	2. D	2. A
3. B	3. A	3. D	3. C	3. B
4. D	4. D	4. D	4. A	4. D
5. A	5. C	5. B	5. A	5. C
	6. A	6. B		

WEEK 10

DAY 1	DAY 2	DAY 3	DAY 4	DAY 5
1. D	1. B	1. C	1. A	1. D
2. B	2. A	2. B	2. B	2. B
3. D	3. A	3. A	3. B	3. C
4. A	4. D	4. D	4. C	4. D
5. B	5. C	5. C	5. D	5. B
6. D	6. B	6. A	6. B	6. A

WEEK 11

DAY 1	DAY 2	DAY 3	DAY 4	DAY 5
1. A	1. C	1. A	1. C	1. A
2. D	2. B	2. B	2. B	2. D
3. C	3. D	3. D	3. A	3. B
4. D	4. A	4. C	4. D	4. A
5. B	5. D	5. D	5. B	5. B
				6. C

WEEK 12

DAY 1	DAY 2	DAY 3	DAY 4	DAY 5
1. C	1. C	1. C	1. D	1. B
2. D	2. D	2. D	2. C	2. C
3. C	3. D	3. D	3. A	3. B
4. B	4. A	4. B	4. A	4. A
5. A	5. D	5. C	5. A	5. B
6. B		6. D		

ANSWER KEY

WEEK 13

DAY 1	DAY 2	DAY 3	DAY 4	DAY 5
1. D	1. B	1. A	1. A	1. D
2. C	2. C	2. B	2. B	2. A
3. C	3. D	3. D	3. D	3. B
4. A	4. D	4. C	4. C	4. A
5. B	5. C	5. C	5. B	5. D
6. D	6. D	6. C	6. C	

WEEK 14

DAY 1	DAY 2	DAY 3	DAY 4	DAY 5
1. B	1. A	1. D	1. A	1. D
2. C	2. B	2. C	2. B	2. C
3. A	3. B	3. A	3. C	3. D
4. D	4. A	4. D	4. D	4. B
5. C	5. D	5. B	5. B	5. A
6. D	6. B			

WEEK 15

DAY 1	DAY 2	DAY 3	DAY 4	DAY 5
1. D	1. C	1. D	1. B	1. B
2. B	2. A	2. A	2. A	2. A
3. A	3. A	3. C	3. C	3. A
4. B	4. D	4. A	4. D	4. C
5. B	5. B	5. C	5. D	5. C

WEEK 16

DAY 1	DAY 2	DAY 3	DAY 4	DAY 5
1. A	1. B	1. D	1. A	1. A
2. C	2. C	2. A	2. C	2. C
3. B	3. B	3. B	3. B	3. D
4. A	4. D	4. C	4. D	4. D
5. C	5. D	5. B	5. C	5. A
6. D				

WEEK 17

DAY 1	DAY 2	DAY 3	DAY 4	DAY 5
1. C	1. C	1. B	1. D	1. B
2. B	2. A	2. D	2. C	2. A
3. A	3. A	3. D	3. B	3. B
4. A	4. B	4. C	4. A	4. C
5. C	5. A	5. C	5. C	5. A

WEEK 18

DAY 1	DAY 2	DAY 3	DAY 4	DAY 5
1. C	1. D	1. D	1. C	1. D
2. B	2. B	2. D	2. A	2. C
3. C	3. C	3. B	3. B	3. A
4. C	4. A	4. A	4. A	4. D
5. B	5. B	5. A	5. D	5. A
6. C				

ANSWER KEY

WEEK 19

	DAY 1	DAY 2	DAY 3	DAY 4	DAY 5
1.	C	D	B	D	B
2.	C	B	C	C	A
3.	B	A	A	A	A
4.	C	B	B	D	C
5.	D	A	B	C	D

WEEK 20

	DAY 1	DAY 2	DAY 3	DAY 4	DAY 5
1.	C	C	D	C	D
2.	D	D	B	A	C
3.	A	C	C	C	D
4.	B	B	A	B	A
5.	C	A	D	D	B

CHALLENGE QUESTIONS

WEEK 1

$50,000

WEEK 2

2,700

WEEK 3

20

WEEK 4

$1,012

WEEK 5

120

WEEK 6

22

WEEK 7

Answers may vary but should have 2 models (bars, circles, etc.)
The models should have the same amounts shaded.
Correct answers may look like the model to the right.

WEEK 8

$4\frac{7}{8}$ pounds

WEEK 9

$5\frac{7}{20}$ hours

WEEK 10

$0.36

WEEK 11

0.7 > 0.46

WEEK 12

52 ounces

WEEK 13

900 feet
or 300 yards

WEEK 14

Whole Watermelons Eaten

0	$\frac{1}{8}$	$\frac{1}{4}$	$\frac{3}{8}$	$\frac{1}{2}$	$\frac{5}{8}$	$\frac{3}{4}$	$\frac{7}{8}$	$\frac{8}{8}$

WEEK 15

1,080

WEEK 16

98°

WEEK 17

The angles in a triangle add up to 180 degrees.

WEEK 18

112°

WEEK 19

Parallelogram or rhombus

WEEK 20

Circles have an unlimited number of lines of symmetry.

1. A
2. C
3. B
4. D
5. B
6. C
7. D
8. A
9. C
10. B
11. B
12. B
13. D
14. A
15. D
16. C
17. B
18. C
19. D
20. C
21. A
22. B

23. C
24. C
25. B
26. D
27. A
28. D
29. C
30. 6
31. 90 yards
32. $\frac{36}{5}$ or $7\frac{1}{5}$
33. 1,2,3,4,6,8,12,24
34. 34 and 46
35. $(4\times100,000) + (3\times1000) + (6\times100) + (2\times10) + (9\times1)$
36. $\frac{4}{5} < \frac{9}{10}$
37. AXB = 180 – 90 – 78 or AXB = 180 – (90 + 78)
38. Acute angles should be < 90°
    Right angles should be 90°
    Obtuse angles should be > 90°

39.

40. 36 and 96 inches
41. 7,650 feet
42. Angles have 2 rays with a common endpoint.

43.

44. $6\frac{4}{5}$ gallons
45. $7\frac{1}{2}$ pounds

COMMON CORE TEST SERIES

The goal of these workbooks is to provide mock state tests so students can increase confidence and test scores during actual test day.

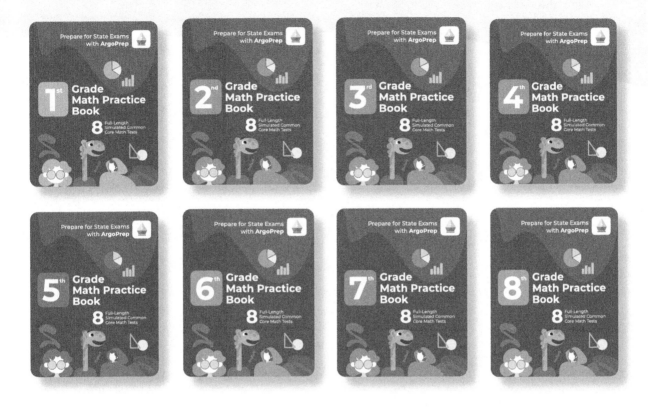

FrogYogi Math Series

It combines fun and engaging activities along with math concepts. Your child will be hooked in learning math on a daily basis. This workbook includes fun and effective yoga math breaks between solving problems helping the brain relax and retain more information.

Made in the USA
Middletown, DE
08 January 2021